FAITH & REASON(S)

CONFRONTING POPULAR OPINION WITH GOD'S TRUTH

BY JOE CADY

TABLE OF CONTENTS

FOREWORD
BY MARK HART

One Saturday when I was in middle school my father entered my room, turned off my television and video game system and told me to follow him into the garage. Never mind that I was on the verge of a high score or that the entire galaxy's peace and freedom hung in the balance… alas, I obediently followed my father out of respect (and fear for my life should I decline).

On that weekend and on countless to follow my father began walking me through the finer points of an automobile and — more to the point — automotive maintenance. He demonstrated how to use jumper cables and taught me how to remove and setup a jack. Side by side he showed me how to change a tire, to survey the battery water, and change spark plugs. He explained the importance of the oil, how to check it and how to change it, when needed.

This is the part where I'd love to say that I was a great sport about the lessons. I'd love to say that I sat attentively listening to each session or that I enjoyed the extra time with my father. I did not. I was too great of a brat to fully comprehend what a gift my father was giving to me. "I won't have a license for another three years, Dad," I would complain. "What's the point of doing this when I don't even own a car?" I lamented. "Why can't I just hang out inside and you can show me this stuff in a few years?" I whined.

My father, however, understood something that I had yet to learn in my youthful omnipotence… namely, that when you *need* to know something important for survival, it's often too late to learn it. How prophetic my father was when I found myself — at 14 years old — on the side of a road with my friend, his mom, and her defunct minivan en route to a baseball game we'd never make. They sat and watched in heroic amazement as I leapt into action, changing that tire like I was working pit crew at the Indy 500. How timely my father's teachings were on countless occasions in grocery store parking lots, on Church retreats, and even on one groom's wedding day when others were unable to diagnose or fix his automotive issues. My father shared wisdom, and in doing so, he had given me the gift of practical knowledge; that knowledge proved to save not only my behind, but countless others' in the process.

In a way, this book, *Faith and Reason(s)* is a lot like what my father did for me. In the pages that follow you will be given an invaluable gift, one that will undoubtedly bless you and many others for years to come. The author, Joe Cady, is more than a good friend, he is a skilled teacher who not only knows the content but who cares about your soul. Joe is a trusted guide with a servant heart and his desire is pure — he wants to help you get to heaven.

We live in an age where information is shared instantly and readily. Virtually any idea or fact is immediately accessible from almost anywhere in the world from the palm of your hand. With so much information available, however, it becomes even more important that what we read is from a trusted source. In an age where anyone with a latte and a blog can take a swing at God, His truth, and His Church (as many do), how do we as His children not only learn *who* to listen to for truth but *how* to communicate said truth to a culture so in need of it?

Put simply, you were born into a self-proclaimed "enlightened" culture that is steeped in darkness. You were born in a time and into an era where those entrusted to teach and spread truth, most especially on the high school and university campuses, are largely atheistic and increasingly antagonistic about it.

So how does the modern Christian not only wade through misconceptions and half-truths, but learn to articulate the fullness of God's truth entrusted to and revealed within His Church? How do *you* allow the light of Christ, burning within you by virtue of the sacraments, to burn even brighter in this universe of "dark matter" that science has so skillfully "explained" without explaining anything at all? Our ancient ancestors would lie beneath the blanket of stars, look up at the night sky and proclaim it "the heavens"; modern minds peer up and label it "space." Who sounds more enlightened and who sounds "blind" in that moment?

The more that modern minds try to scientifically make everything "lucid," the more everything becomes mysterious and unsolvable. As the great Catholic thinker and writer G.K. Chesterton pointed out in his book *Orthodoxy*, the Christian "allows one thing to be mysterious and everything else becomes lucid." When we allow God to be God, everything is ordered and makes sense, but when we attempt to remove the Creator from creation, creation becomes disordered. We seek God in faith and allow our understanding to catch up. St. Anselm (and later St. Thomas Aquinas) wrote and spoke in great detail about this, calling it *"fides quaerens intellectum"* from the Latin for "faith seeking understanding." St. Anselm demonstrated that faith did not contradict reason but, rather, that faith exceeded mere human reason. He set out to convince the "foolish souls" who had "said in his heart, 'There is no God'" (Psalm 14:1, 53:1). As a modern follower of Christ, you are being asked to do the same.

In the pages that follow, Joe is going help your faith grow in understanding. He will give you the inestimable gift of perspective. He will treat a dozen of the most common "problems" and rebuttals people offer in conversations and online as to why they could never be part of Christ's Church or why there is no God in their opinion or why religion is like a four-letter word in their estimation. This book will not only help you understand the correct answers but will help you help others discern the right question(s). As modeled by our Lord Jesus, Himself, the virtue of prudence is not as much about giving another every answer as much as it is helping them to ask the correct question (see John 18:37; Luke 7:44; Matthew 23:24; Mark 5:39).

In each chapter, Joe will take you into the garage of modern philosophical and theological thought. He'll walk you through the engine of thought employed by many moderns, show you where things have a tendency to break down, and tell you what is important to keep this vehicle of truth moving forward. How thankful your friends and family will be — many of whom might lack basic (theological) automotive knowledge — when they find themselves stranded and lost and you are there to offer practical and timely help.

There will be no shortage of competing voices in your life offering their "take" on truth whether online, in a classroom, or around a dinner table. Be careful who you choose to listen to and pay attention to how their own wounds, struggles and ignorance can allow popular opinion to overtake unpopular truth in their personal decision making. As Jesus warned us, "If the blind follow the blind, they both will fall into the pit" (Matthew 15:14).

One last thought before you turn this page… you will see a variety of responses when you share truth with people. When the soul of another has grown accustomed to and comfortable within the darkness, voices of light are not only unwelcome, they are unappreciated. Do not be deterred. The truth has to be shared and if not by you, by whom? Sharing Christ's light with others requires both mercy and patience. Hearts blinded by evil's lies require time to dilate. Some will be open to the Church's wisdom (Acts 8) and some will not (Acts 17), but the truth of Christ is unchanging and eternal (Hebrews 13:8) and offers freedom (John 8:32).

Ironically, some of the greatest saints, martyrs, and evangelists began as the fiercest adversaries to the Church in their time. The soul who most desperately needs the Church's truth is the one the Lord places right in front of you. So keep this book nearby. Refer back to it often. Share it with others. Get away from the screens and spend some time in the theological garage with a masterful mechanic. Learn, as I did, that it's not just about knowing bits and pieces of truth, picking and choosing what interests you when you feel like it; it's about understanding the whole so you can understand and explain the parts to others, when they are most in need.

So pray now, that your hearts will be open as you read and that the hearts of those who the Lord will place before you in the coming months and years will likewise be open to His timeless truth. While you cannot control where life's roads will take you, you can feel confident that the Holy Spirit is in the driver's seat and that your car is built to last no matter what comes your way.

Happy motoring.

Mark Hart
Executive Vice President, Life Teen

CHAPTER 1

HOW DO WE KNOW GOD EXISTS?

The enormity of this question cannot be denied. Deciding where we stand on the "does God exist?" issue is the ultimate fork in the road. How we answer it will in many ways determine the very direction of our lives. The question of God's existence is one of those primary questions that everyone in some way has to consider at some point in their lives. But there are really two parts to this question:

(1) Does God exist?
(2) How do we *know* that God exists?

Now, before answering these questions, we have to be very clear about one thing: The answer to the first question "Does God exist?" is either "yes" or "no." There is no room for any of this "That may be true for you but not for me" nonsense. God either exists or He doesn't... period! Even if we have no way of knowing it, the statement "There is a God" is either true or false. When one person says, "I believe in God," and another says, "I don't believe in God," it's possible for both of *those* statements to be true (i.e., it can be true that one person really does *believe* in God and also true that the other really does not *believe* in God). However, the statements "There is a God" and "There is no God" cannot both be true. Either there is a God, or there is not. Therefore, in all of the discussions and disagreements about the question of God's existence, we must always keep in mind that there is a definitive fact of the matter: God either exists or He doesn't, it can't be both.

You might be thinking, *That's great, but we are still left with our original two questions: "Does God exist?" and "How do we know that God exists?"* In regard to the first question (which, remember, can only have a "yes" or "no" answer but not both), the Catholic Church of course says, "YES!" This belief forms the basis of Christianity; everything else that Christians believe ultimately makes no sense if there is no God. Belief in God is so fundamental to the Faith that our two basic creeds begin with the words "I believe in God." But here's the thing: Just because people *believe* that God exists doesn't mean that God actually does exist. So, the question remains: How do we *know* whether or not there actually is a God? What are the reasons that people give to justify their belief in God?

THE EXISTENCE OF GOD

Countless books have been written attempting to prove that God exists — far too many to discuss here. The most basic arguments start with the physical world, what we can see and experience around us, and reason backward toward their ultimate cause. The idea is really very simple. Whenever you come across something in the world, a very natural question to ask is, "Where did this come from?"

Nothing just appears. There is a reason why things exist; they are *made*.

Take a car, for example. When you go to buy a car, do you say to yourself, *Man, aren't I lucky that all these pieces of metal, plastic, rubber, and electronics came together randomly in just the right way to function as a car?* Of course not. Obviously, the car was made. Someone (actually, a lot of people) used their skill and intelligence to first design the plans for the car and then actually work to bring about its existence. And the same is true of the parts themselves; they, too, were planned, designed, and made with a purpose.

> "The existence of God the Creator can be known with certainty through His works, by the light of human reason, even if this knowledge is often obscured and disfigured by error" (*CCC* 286).

But what about the people who made them — where did they come from? Well, no individual is the cause of his or her own existence. Everyone has a mother and a father who provide an explanation for why he or she is here. But what about that person's mom and dad? Where did they come from? Well, from *their* parents. But what about them? (Can you see where this is going?) At some point, we are left with a question: What started all of this? Where did everything ultimately come from?

Well, the options are: either there is a Creator who is the cause and reason for everything that exists, or... what? Things have just always been there? Does this really provide a satisfying answer? What about the answer that everything came from an initial "big bang"? We will be looking into the question of creation versus evolution in chapter 9, but for now we can ask the question: What about this "thing" that supposedly exploded in the big bang theory — where did *that* come from? There must be something that got the whole thing moving in the first place. And whatever this *thing* is, it would have to be something with the power to create and the wisdom to do it in a way that works. I mean, just consider the fact that if the earth were spinning even slightly faster or slower, our planet could not sustain life — we would all go flying off into space. Does it seem more reasonable to think that this is just a lucky coincidence or that the speed of the earth's rotation is what it is precisely because it was designed for the purpose of sustaining life?

GOD AS FIRST CAUSE

When we look at the nature of cause and effect, we are left with two reasonable conclusions:

(1) There must be some *first cause* that is the source of everything else that exists. As we said before, nothing just comes into existence by its own effort or intention. You aren't here because you decided to be; you are here because of a particular reason and cause. (You see, when a man and a woman love each other... You know what? Go ask your mom.) When we keep going back in time to ask, "But what is the cause of this; where did this come from?" we are left with a long series of causes that ultimately has to have begun with something, some *first cause*. And this *first cause* is what we would call God.

"In different ways, man can come to know that there exists a reality which is the first cause and final end of all things, a reality that everyone calls God" (*CCC* 34).

But here's the thing: We shouldn't think of God as one being among many, as if God were just a super-being among other beings. No, God doesn't *have* being; He *IS* being. God isn't one existing thing among many — He is *existence itself*. Is your head spinning now? Put simply, everything else that exists in some way shares in the being that God Himself is... in His very nature. This is why it really doesn't make sense to ask, "Who made God?" or "Where did God come from?" God just *is*, and He always has been. There's never been a time

"God is the fullness of Being and of every perfection, without origin and without end. All creatures receive all that they are and have from Him; but He alone is His very being, and He is of Himself everything that He is" (*CCC* 213).

when God "wasn't." He is the source and cause of all else that exists. For more on this, check out the *Catechism of the Catholic Church* on God creating out of nothing (*CCC* 212–213, 296–298).

(2) This *first cause* must be something (or someone) powerful and intelligent, able to create a complex and ordered universe. When we look at the world, we see great complexity in how things function and interact. As a result, we are led to the reasonable conclusion that things function the way they do because of an intentional design of the Creator. This is what happens when we come across things that are man-made, isn't it? No one looks at things like smartphones, airplanes, or watches and thinks that their complexity and inner workings are the result of chance or coincidence. So why would we think this when we look at the universe as a whole? In our everyday experience, an intelligent, ordered design naturally leads us to conclude that these things are the result of an intelligent designer, with the wisdom and power to create. Why should it be any different with regard to the universe as a whole? God's wisdom and power is seen in what He has made. As it says in Scripture, "For from the greatness and the beauty of created things their original author, by analogy, is seen" (Wisdom 13:5).

"Created in God's image and called to know and love Him, the person who seeks God discovers certain ways of coming to know Him. These are also called proofs for the existence of God, not in the sense of proofs in the natural sciences, but rather in the sense of converging and convincing arguments which allow us to attain certainty about the truth" (*CCC* 31).

The point of all this is to show that belief in God is not simply some blind impulse or imposed doctrine. Belief in God is reasonable and evident when we look at the created world. And it is this reasonableness that is at the heart of the various arguments for God's existence.

HOW DO WE VIEW GOD?

Let's consider for a second why people often don't believe in God. There is a good chance that for most people the issue isn't that they haven't been presented with a convincing philosophical argument to prove God's existence. So what is it? One common reason is the existence of evil and suffering, which for many people poses a serious roadblock to faith in a good and loving God (we will look at this in the next chapter). But another reason people don't believe in God is because of the way God is portrayed to them. For example, many people get the impression that God is not a loving God who actually wants what is best for them, but a God who looks down upon a sinful world and is angry. Not only is such an image a barrier to believing in God, it is actually a false image. God is love. And everything that God does is motivated out of love — nothing else.

It is true that we are sinners, and it is true that sin is contrary to God's will and design for His people. But if Christians' first message to others is that we are sinners who need to escape God's wrath, not only will we be very ineffective, we will also rob the Gospel of its full meaning. We have to start first with God's love. God created us simply because He is good, and it is the very nature of goodness to want to share itself. God didn't *need* us; He *wanted* us so that we might fully experience the love and goodness that He Himself *is*. This is the beginning of the story; we were made *by* love and *for* love. Only after this point is made can we begin to speak of sin. God hates sin, but not because it makes Him mad. God hates sin because it is *bad for us*. And God is opposed to anything that might prevent us from fully experiencing the love for which we were created.

This is why God gives us commandments to follow. It's not because God is a control freak who wants to dictate our every move, but because He wants to show us a path that leads to life, love, and goodness (more on this in chapter 6). The fact of the matter is that we aren't sinners in the hands of an angry God; we are lost children of a loving Father. The problem with sin isn't that it makes God hate us, but that it hinders in us our very ability to know the God who couldn't possibly love us any more. It is this understanding of God that Jesus came to reveal and that Christians must carry into the world. Faith in God is reasonable and can be explained with logical arguments, but unless Christians faithfully present God as a loving Father who wants to restore us to the fullness of life and love that He intended, the strength of our reasoned arguments will only go so far.

> "God's very being is love. By sending His only Son and the Spirit of Love in the fullness of time, God has revealed His innermost secret: God Himself is an eternal exchange of love, Father, Son, and Holy Spirit, and He has destined us to share in that exchange" (*CCC* 221).

CHAPTER 2

IF THERE IS A GOD, WHY IS THERE SO MUCH EVIL AND SUFFERING IN THE WORLD?

When you look at the world and see all the instances of suffering and injustice, it is very natural and reasonable to ask, "Why?" Why would a loving God allow things like hurricanes, tsunamis, or droughts? Whether it is you, someone you know, or even a stranger on the news, when we see and experience suffering in the world, we want an explanation. For many people, an experience of intense and seemingly meaningless suffering (such as an illness or the death of a child) leads them to abandon their faith in God. It is also true that most people who identify themselves as atheists use examples of suffering as evidence to support their belief that God does not exist. Therefore, we must not minimize the seriousness of this question.

Obviously there *is* suffering and evil in the world. Any response to the question of why must start with an honest acknowledgment of this reality. It is something we simply cannot escape as we pass through life. And so, our response must not be understood as minimizing or taking lightly the reality of suffering, but rather answering the question of whether the presence of such suffering proves that God does not exist.

WHY IS THERE SUFFERING?

Ultimately, the answer to the question of the existence of evil and suffering cannot be separated from God's plan to overcome and save us from sin and death. No sufficient answer to this question can be given apart from Jesus Christ, who came to set us free from evil. But before getting into that, we must begin with an acknowledgment that the world is not as it ought to be. What do we mean by this? In the first chapters of the book of Genesis

"We must approach the question of the origin of evil by fixing the eyes of our faith on Him who alone is its conqueror" (*CCC* 385).

(Genesis 1-3) we get an account of God creating the world and the first human beings. Now, these chapters cannot be taken as historical or scientific records of *how* the world was made (nor were they intended to be). Instead, these words were written to reveal theological truths about God, creation, and its relationship to Him. Therefore, the accounts of God creating the world in seven days and the story of Adam and Eve must be read with this question in mind: What does this tell us about God, ourselves, and God's plan for creation? If you haven't read the story, you may want to pause here and read Genesis 1 through 3 (it won't take you very long).

Christianity has understood these chapters to reveal a number of important things:

(1) All creation was made out of love and for the purpose of sharing in the love and goodness of God. God had no other reason for creating than His desire to share with us what He, Himself, is — an eternal communion of love. God, in His essence, is a relationship. You might even say, God is a family, but the most perfect, loving family you can imagine. And the reason He made us was so that we could experience life in this family.

> "The inner harmony of the human person, the harmony between man and woman, and finally the harmony between the first couple and all creation, comprised the state called original justice" (*CCC* 376).

(2) God intended for us to live in harmony with Himself, each other, and all creation. When God made our first parents, they were created in this harmony, which the *Catechism* calls "original justice." God intended for things to stay this way; as long as humanity remained faithful to God, there would be no suffering or death.

(3) Sin and disobedience changed everything. Through the sin of our first parents, this harmony was lost, and all creation fell out of whack. You see, the sin of Adam and Eve didn't just affect them; it wounded their very nature, and from that point forward, all humanity (as well as all creation) would exist in a fallen state. This is why we call Adam and Eve's sin "the fall" — our first parents *fell* from the grace of sharing in God's own life.

So, where does this leave us? Well, regardless of the details of the story, the truth revealed is clear. God created us for life — to live in harmony with Him and each other. Sin, however, disrupted this plan. Sin brought chaos and disorder to a world that God created to experience harmony and unity. As a result of this sin, suffering and death are now part of picture.

WHAT EXACTLY IS SIN?

Sin is not breaking some rule that God has arbitrarily set in place to control us. To sin is to act in a way contrary to love. To sin is to act in a disordered way. What do we mean by disordered? Well, our freedom and will were given to us as gifts from God so that we could *freely choose* what is good. Our freedom is ordered to choose things that are truly good. True freedom doesn't mean doing whatever we want; true freedom is only rightly exercised when it freely embraces what is good, beautiful, and true. And so, what God and the Church call sins are those things that move us away from what is truly good, beautiful, and true. Sin is disordered because it is a misuse of our freedom, a freedom that was given specifically for the sake of embracing the good. Ultimately, sin is failing to act in the way love and goodness require. The Greek word for *sin* literally means, "to miss the mark." When we sin, we fail to hit our intended target: goodness, beauty, and truth.

> "Freedom consists not in doing what we like, but in having the right to do what we ought" (John Paul II).

SIN AND SUFFERING

Suffering and death are ultimately the result of sin, a disordered use of human freedom. This is easier to see in the case of *moral evil* (evil done by human beings), but not always so clear in the case of *natural evil* (such as earthquakes and illness). In the case of moral evil, we can see that when we use our freedom in ways that are contrary to what is good and true (for example, out of anger, greed, or lust), our actions bring about evil and suffering. But what about natural evil? Well, mysteriously God has tied the fate of the world to the fate of humanity. And so, with the fall of Adam and Eve, all creation fell into decay and disorder, which has resulted in sickness, disaster, and death.

Suffering and evil are realities that we must face in life, and they are all in some way tied to the sin and disobedience that brings disorder and death to creation. But the question remains: Couldn't God have created a world free from suffering and evil? Well, the answer is actually "yes." God could have created a better world, but in His wisdom He chose to create *this* world. Why God did not do otherwise is something Christians have wrestled with throughout history.

In answering this question, the common response has basically been that God allows evil because He knows that He is able to bring good out of it. God doesn't desire or intend evil, but He does permit it, because He knows how to work in and through it for the good of His children. (Check out quotes from various saints in the *Catechism* on this issue, especially 313 and 412.) Now, this probably won't satisfy those who see the presence of suffering in the world as a reason to not believe in God. There is an important piece of the puzzle missing, however, and that is Jesus Christ. We know that God sent His own Son into our fallen, wounded world with all its suffering for the sake of overcoming evil. Jesus came to restore us to the life and goodness that God intended for us from the beginning. Jesus Himself came and walked the path of our humanity, and He experienced suffering and evil just as we do. For this reason the Church says we cannot even attempt to answer questions about suffering without looking at the life and mission of Jesus.

JESUS: LIKE US IN ALL THINGS BUT SIN

Jesus knows what it's like to experience the suffering and evil of this world. He knew poverty, the death of loved ones, betrayal, unjust accusation, violence, gossip, abandonment by friends in a time of need, and temptation. And He ultimately experienced intense suffering and death at the hands of the very people He came to save. And yet, God used all of this to show the power of love over sin, the power of life over death.

You see, Jesus came into a fallen world and experienced the extreme effects of a world disordered by sin (exemplified in the crucifixion) and triumphed over it by the power of love, a selfless and sacrificial love that gives life to the world. In Jesus we see the ultimate example of God's ability to bring good out of evil. In the sacrificial life and death of Christ, we see that suffering and death is not the end of the story. In short, we see in Jesus that even when all looks dark and hopeless, life and love have the final word if we trust in our loving Father. Because we have a God who has endured the pain and suffering of the world and came out triumphant, we can turn to Him in our time of need.

"Cast all your worries upon Him because He cares for you" (1 Peter 5:7).

When we unite our sufferings to His, God can mysteriously use them in life-changing ways.

This is why John Paul II said that when we are in the midst of suffering and asking the question "Why me?" we must turn to Jesus and see that "the one to whom we put to question is Himself suffering and wishes to answer us from the Cross, from the heart of His own suffering" (*Salvifici Doloris*, 26). But Christ's suffering and death can never be separated from His Resurrection, where He shows us the power of life and love over sin and death. This is what Christ proves to us, and this is why Mother Teresa said, "Never let anything so fill you with sorrow as to make you forget the joy of the Risen Christ" (*Life in the Spirit*, 63).

When it comes down to it, we can't explain why suffering happens in each and every case — and this inability to explain it is part of what makes suffering so painful — but what we do know is that we are not alone in our suffering. God Himself is a compassionate God, who sent His own Son into the world to suffer with it and provide a passage from death to life. When our suffering is united to Christ, our suffering can be redemptive, meaning that God can use it to bring about good. Suffering and evil are real, but so are love and goodness, and the light of love can never be overcome by the darkness of evil.

CHAPTER 3

I'M SPIRITUAL BUT NOT RELIGIOUS.

For many people today, "religion" is a dirty word. They are generally fine with words like "spirituality," and might even tolerate a concept like God, but as soon as religion enters the stage, people start to get uncomfortable. There seems to be a general acceptance of spiritual ideas, just as long as no one starts talking about religion specifically. Religion (many claim) complicates things and gets people caught up in doctrine and morals, when what really matters is "discovering the divine within yourself" or "connecting with the sacred energy of the cosmos" (the language is varied, but the idea is usually the same: Being spiritual means being connected in some way with the spirit, soul, divine, etc., without any ties to a specific religion). This is why one of the most common labels people give themselves when identifying their "religious affiliation" is "spiritual, but not religious." Many modern minds are quick to identify themselves as connected in some way to some higher power or sacred energy, but it is less common for people to identify themselves with a specific organized religion.

So, what's the problem? Well, the main problem is that most forms of the "spiritual but not religious" mentality are simply spiritualities of one's own making — a user-friendly, this-works-for-me spirituality. Very often being "spiritual but not religious" means picking this or that aspect of various religions, beliefs, and practices and building them up into a self-made system — a sort of do-it-yourself spirituality suited to one's own desires. But there is one problem with this: It completely sidesteps the question of *truth*. Are all spiritual paths of equal value? Are there beliefs, practices, and worldviews that reflect reality more accurately than others? These questions will be looked at further in the next chapter, but for now, let's take a closer look at the statement itself. What does it mean, and is it true?

When people describe themselves as spiritual, what they usually mean is that they are interested in spiritual things. This could mean an interest in the soul, the supernatural, the divine (however that is understood), the interconnectedness of the cosmos, etc. According to this understanding, one person might describe themselves as spiritual while another may not, depending upon their interest in these sorts of things. But when Christians use the term spiritual to describe

> "Spirit and matter, in man, are not two natures united, but rather their union forms a single nature" (CCC 365).

a person, they are saying this as a matter of *fact* and in a universal sense.

This is because the Christian understanding of "spiritual" is different. You see, a fundamental belief of Christianity is that human beings are unique in all of creation, and what makes humans unique is the fact that they are a union of body and soul. To be human means to have a unified body and soul in one human nature. So, in this sense, Christianity would say that every human being is spiritual. By the mere fact that they are human, they share in both the material and spiritual realm (see *CCC* 327). From the perspective of the Church, being "spiritual" is not an option; one doesn't decide to be spiritual. One simply *is* spiritual, by one's very nature. What makes us humans different from all other material things is that we have been created with a spiritual soul. Human beings are not just physical objects; they are the unique combination of body and soul, material and spiritual. Therefore, we can't *choose* to be spiritual any more than we can choose to have arms and legs. Being spiritual is simply part of what it means to be human.

Admittedly, this isn't what people generally mean when they call themselves spiritual. As we saw above, usually what is meant is simply an interest in spirituality or spiritual things. However, it is important to understand that the Church has a particular concept of what it means to be a *spiritual being*. When the Church calls people spiritual, it is a statement about our nature, not our interests.

"I SEE THAT YOU ARE VERY SPIRITUAL"

If we define *spiritual* in the interested-in-spirituality sense, how do we respond to people who identify themselves as such? Saint Paul provides us with a great response in the Acts of the Apostles. While traveling in Greece and seeing the numerous statues in honor of the Greek pantheon, St. Paul came to realize that the Greeks were very "religious" people. Although he used the word "religious," what he recognized in the Greeks was a deep interest in the divine or supernatural realm. In this sense, it could be fair to say that St. Paul recognized them to be very *spiritual* people. What did St. Paul do? He began his speech with the words, "You Athenians, I see that in every respect you are very religious" (Acts 17:22). Now, was St. Paul criticizing them here? No! He affirmed in them something that is ultimately good.

The fact of the matter is that people *are* spiritual, and not just because they are made up of body and soul. People are spiritual (in the sense of being interested in spiritual things) because each and every one of us was made for union with a spiritual being. All of us were made to know and love something that lies beyond the natural world, which is what "supernatural" means.

When people recognize this longing and identify it, they are recognizing something really present within them, which is ultimately a desire for God (even if they don't call it this). When people say that they are spiritual, we should say, "You're right!" All of us are spiritual because we are all searching for a meaning for life that can only be found outside of ourselves.

> "The desire for God is written in the human heart, because man is created by God and for God; and God never ceases to draw man to Himself. Only in God will he find the truth and happiness he never stops searching for" (*CCC* 27).

There is nothing wrong with being spiritual, and like St. Paul, we ought to affirm this spiritual sensitivity in others as a good thing. But we should also be ready to do what St. Paul does next, which is to identify God as the very thing for which people are searching. If we continue reading in the Acts of the Apostles, we hear St. Paul say:

> "For as I passed along, and observed the objects of your worship, I found also an altar with this inscription, 'To an unknown god.' What therefore you worship as unknown, this I proclaim to you. The God who made the world and everything in it, being Lord of heaven and earth, does not live in shrines made by man, nor is He served by human hands, as though He needed anything, since He Himself gives to all men life and breath and everything" (Acts 17:23–25).

Our interest in spiritual things will only be satisfied in God, and not just God in a general sense but God revealed to us as Father, Son, and Holy Spirit, which we'll cover more in the next chapter.

DON'T CALL ME RELIGIOUS!

What about the question of being religious? This is where it gets tricky because, while some people might specifically say that they are not religious, the Church would say that *everyone* is religious.

Of course, just like the word "spiritual," the Church has a particular understanding of what it means to be "religious." What most people mean when they say they are not religious is that they don't identify themselves with an organized religion. Their reason for not clinging to any particular religion is that they claim that God — or the goddess, or the divine, or whatever — can't be confined to any religious system. What's interesting is that this view is found both inside and outside of Christianity. There are many Christians who would say they have a real, personal relationship with Jesus but are not part of organized Christian religion ("It's about a relationship, not a religion" is their motto).

When the Church says that everyone is religious, it means that human beings, specifically because they are made up of body and spirit, seek to give concrete expression to their universal longing for the divine. The Church would say that human beings are *by nature* religious beings, and that the variety of religious expressions throughout time and culture is evidence of this.

You see, because we experience reality though our humanness (through our five senses), we have a natural tendency to give concrete expression to our ideas and beliefs. This is why Jesus instituted the sacraments in the Church. It wasn't because *He* needed them; He knew *we* needed them. And so Christ chose to use things we could see, touch, taste, and smell to communicate to us the grace that we cannot see or touch. In a sense, God gave us the sacraments because humans are ultimately sacramental by nature (that is, inclined to attach meaning to physical actions and signs). Just look at the ritual surrounding the opening ceremonies for the Olympics. We create all sorts of symbols and gestures to represent our unity across national lines, our interconnectedness, our commitment to respect and good sportsmanship, and other concepts we value. This reveals something very interesting about us: We are ritualistic people who respond to repetition and symbolic expression.

> "In many ways, throughout history down to the present day, men have given expression to their quest for God in their religious beliefs and behavior. These forms of religious expression, despite the ambiguities they often bring with them, are so universal that one may well call man a religious being" (*CCC* 28).

This is so much a part of our lives that we often don't even realize it. Consider the last time you dressed up in a tux or a fancy dress, or the last time you ate with "the good china," or the last time you shook someone's hand. In each of these things, our actions are meant to communicate something; our ideas and sentiments are given concrete expression in ritual. And it is in this sense that all humanity can be described as religious. (For more on this, check out *CCC* 1146–1148.)

AN ASSESSMENT

So what about the statement "I'm spiritual but not religious"? It might be true that those who say this do not identify themselves with any specific religious institution; they may even have some sort of opposition to such institutions. But it can't be true that they are not religious in the way the Church understands it. Everyone, even those who would not call themselves religious, are ritualistic — using time, space, symbols, and gestures to give meaning and expression to their ideas and sentiments. Therefore, when someone says that they are not religious, or that they reject religion, what they are really saying is that they reject this or that religion, or that they reject a particular ritual or system of religious expression.

However, if we are really honest, saying, "I'm spiritual but not religious" is nothing more than saying, "I'm religious, but it's on my own terms... no one tells me what my spiritual quest should look like." And when we say that God cannot be limited or confined to one system of religious belief and expression, are we saying that all religions are of equal value?

Such a view leaves unresolved the burning question brought up earlier: Is there any "religious path" that is better or truer than another? This is precisely what we will consider next.

CHAPTER 4

ALL PATHS LEAD TO GOD, RIGHT?

It is shocking how widespread this view is! Even among people who have chosen a particular religious path, there is a general belief that in the end it really doesn't matter what spiritual path a person chooses. No religion is any better or worse than another — what matters is finding one that *works for you*. The problem with this view is that it puts the focus of religion or spirituality on us rather than God. As we saw in the last chapter, the "I'm spiritual but not religious" option is one of the most common labels that people give themselves when describing their religious views. But it's important to see that, while this view contains a valuable truth, it comes with the potential for a serious error. The truth is that self-professed "spiritual" people are responding to a very real desire for something beyond themselves, and this desire is the direct result of being made by God and for God. The danger comes when our efforts to approach God proceed according to our own terms without any regard for the path that God has set before us. This in turn gives rise to a further error — a belief that it doesn't really matter what you believe or do since all paths ultimately lead to God.

> "The desire for God is written in the human heart, because man is created by God and for God; and God never ceases to draw man to Himself" (*CCC* 27).

In our "that may be true for you but not for me" world, telling someone that one path is better than another is anything but socially acceptable. Denying that all paths lead to God is an almost guaranteed way to make people angry, since it means that some people aren't on the right road and all of life's "paths" are *not* equal. This certainly is not a very politically correct view, but the message of the Gospel has *never* been politically correct, and for that reason, Christianity often makes people angry. The Church has always taken very seriously the words of Jesus Christ in the Gospel of John: "I am the way and the truth and the life. No one comes to the Father except through me" (John 14:6). From the beginning, the Church has repeatedly stood behind this truth and proclaimed it to the world. "There is no salvation through anyone else, nor is there any other name under heaven given to the human race by which we are to be saved" (Acts 4:12).

That's quite a claim. But is it true? Is this what the Catholic Church still teaches today? Yes!

SALVATION IN JESUS ALONE

This teaching is clearly stated in a document of the Church called *"The Unicity and Salvific Universality of Jesus Christ and the Church"* (the next time you want to sound smart just name drop that in a conversation... "So I was reading a document on the unicity and salvific universality of Jesus Christ and the Church the other day..."). This document, written in the year 2000, addresses this very question of other religions and the uniqueness of Christianity. And while the document as a whole is worth reading (it reads just like a novel... a theologically dense novel), here are some of the highlights:

The revelation of Jesus Christ is complete and definitive. We have to remember that Jesus is unlike any other religious figure in history. He is not *just* a prophet, or just a teacher of wisdom and morality; He is

"In this definitive Word of His revelation, God has made Himself known in the fullest possible way. He has revealed to mankind who He is" (*Redemptoris Missio,* 5).

God. This is what makes Him unique — He is the Son of God who became man. He is the Word of God who "became flesh and made His dwelling among us" (John 1:14). Why? Because God wanted to reveal Himself in the most concrete way possible. So He became like one of us (for more on Jesus' uniqueness as fully God and fully man, check out *CCC* 464–469). Therefore, in the person of Jesus Christ is found a knowledge of God that is unique in all of history. In the life and ministry of Jesus we don't just learn *about* God, we see *God Himself.* What makes Jesus' message unique is that it's not just a collection of spiritual wisdom or a pattern of moral behavior (although it certainly includes these things), it provides an encounter and a relationship with God Himself, in and through Jesus. Therefore, it is through Jesus Christ alone that God is most fully known. Nothing else in history compares to this.

Jesus said, "Whoever has seen me has seen the Father" (John 14:9).

Jesus Christ is the universal Savior of all mankind. The very heart of Jesus' life and ministry was a rescue mission. The basic truth of revelation is that God made us for life and love, but through sin, humanity became separated from the life God intended for us. Sin is not an essential part of what it means to be human — sin is optional. Think about that, sinning is not in our nature (which is why we can say that Jesus became fully human and yet was without sin). There is nothing printed into our humanity that says we *have* to sin. God made us for life, love, and goodness, not for sin and death. What this means is that when we sin we are actually behaving in a subhuman way. Obviously we don't cease to be human when we sin, but in sinning we act in a way that God never intended. Think of a basketball player. What makes someone a basketball player is the fact that he or she uses skill, speed, and agility to play the game *according to the rules of basketball*. If a player decides to disregard the rules, that player really isn't playing basketball anymore, and in a sense he or she ceases to be a basketball player. In the same way, when we sin, we are disregarding what God has designed us for, which is to love Him and each other.

"Sin is an abuse of the freedom that God gives to created persons so that they are capable of loving Him and loving one another" (*CCC* 387).

When we sin, we simply aren't acting how God has designed us to act. Instead, we are using our freedom and our will in ways that God never intended. To sin is, by nature, to be less than we ought to be. And this sub-human condition is what Jesus came to save us from. Sin, by its very nature, leads to disorder and alienation in our relationship with God, each other, and even within ourselves. Sin disrupts things. It causes relationships to be damaged. It separates and divides people. Sin hurts others (and it hurts us as well).

But remember, God made us for life and love, and so He sent His only Son to overcome all this and restore in us our ability to experience life as God intended. This is uniquely accomplished for all humanity through the life, death, and Resurrection of Jesus Christ — hence the words *unicity* (uniqueness) and *universality* (for everyone) in the title of the Church's document. It is only in and through Jesus, fully divine and fully human, that humanity has been reconciled to God; Jesus "undoes" what we did, and He's the only One Who

"It must be firmly believed as a truth of Catholic faith that the universal salvific will of the One and Triune God is offered and accomplished once for all in the mystery of the Incarnation, death, and Resurrection of the Son of God" (*Dominus Iesus,* 14).

can. This is why the Church has never stopped proclaiming that if anyone is saved, it is by and through Jesus Christ.

This universal plan of salvation is continued in and through the Catholic Church. We know that Jesus came to save us from sin and death, restore us to life, and show us how to love. But this salvation was meant for the entire world. Just like the end zone of every football field reminds us, "For God so loved the world that He sent His only begotten Son" (John 3:16). To make sure that all people would have access to this saving Gospel, He established the Church to be the continuation throughout history of God's saving plan. The Catholic Church isn't just some man-made organization or a general term loosely uniting people who believe in Jesus. The Church is a divinely established institution, sent forth by Christ and empowered by the Holy Spirit to be an instrument of salvation until Jesus comes again. Jesus and the Church cannot be separated. The Church is united to Christ as the instrument through which He continues to accomplish His saving plan.

> "Jesus Christ continues His presence and His work of salvation in the Church and by means of the Church" (*Dominus Iesus*, 16).

These are the central points of the document:

- Jesus is the unique and definitive revelation of God.
- He is the only Savior and means to communion with God.
- He has established the Church to be the continuation of His mission throughout history.

Did you catch all that? In short, the Church is saying that Christianity (specifically Catholicism) provides the fullest and most complete revelation of God the world has ever seen — and Jesus Christ is the only means of salvation for the entire world.

> "Since Christ died for all, and since all men are in fact called to one and the same destiny, which is divine, we must hold that the Holy Spirit offers to all the possibility of being made partners, in a way known to God, in the paschal mystery" (*Gaudium et Spes*, 22).

These two points are as important as any two you will ever learn. So much for all paths leading to God — the Church seems to be saying that there is only one path that leads to God.

If that's the case, what does this mean for those outside the Church? Is everyone who doesn't profess faith in Christ in communion with the Catholic Church out of luck and doomed to be excluded from heaven? Well, interestingly, the Church says "No." The Catholic Church teaches that it *is* possible for those who do not know Christ and His Church to be saved.

So, how do we reconcile the idea that Christ and the Church are necessary for salvation with the idea that it is possible for people outside of the Church to be saved?

Well, the basic idea is that only God knows people's hearts (see 1 Samuel 16:7). Only God knows the extent of someone's faith, or why they are not formally a part of the Church. And we trust that God will judge each person according to the way they have personally responded to His invitation to new life.

You see, there are some people who have never heard of Christ, there are some who have but who don't know that the Catholic Church is necessarily connected to faith in Christ, and there are still others who have heard of Jesus but have never really heard the good news of the Gospel. There are a number of reasons why someone might not publicly profess faith in Jesus and formally join the Catholic Church. But we trust that God is able to save these individuals, too, if they do their best to seek what is true and good throughout life.

> "Those who, through no fault of their own, do not know the Gospel of Christ or His Church, but who nevertheless seek God with a sincere heart, and moved by grace, try in their actions to do His will as they know it through the dictates of their conscience – those too may achieve eternal salvation" (*Lumen Gentium,* 16).

How is this possible? Because anyone who is seriously seeking truth, goodness, and love *is* seeking God. We have faith in a loving and merciful God who alone knows people's hearts and their response to the grace He gives them.

THE SURE PATH

If those who are outside of Catholicism can be saved, does it really matter what you believe? If people on different religious paths are all able to be saved, can't we say that all paths ultimately do lead to God? Well, no. The *possibility* of salvation for those outside the Church does not equal the *assurance* of salvation for those outside the Church.

Think about it this way. Imagine two people heading someplace they have never been before. One has a map and the other doesn't. It is surely possible that both of them could make it to their final destination, but without the map, it's hard to be sure. The person with the map is likely going to get where he is going (if he follows the map correctly), but the person without the map can never really be sure if the path he or she is taking is leading in the right direction. A similar comparison could be made for people in the Church and people outside the Church. Jesus came and essentially said, "*This* is the path to God; if you want life in its fullness, come to Me and I will bring you home." Jesus is the sure path that leads us to our final destination (again, *if* we follow Him). If we want to be sure that we are heading in the right direction, follow the path the God has assured us leads there.

People on some other path may end up making their way to God, but we can't know for sure. God's grace (the help He gives us to follow Him) is always at work drawing people to Himself, and this is true of people both inside and outside the Church. We know that "the hand of the Lord is not too short to save" (Isaiah 59:1). But the fact of the matter is that Jesus came to show us the path of salvation, *so that we could make it*. God *wants* to save us. He *wants* us to make it, and so He gave us a path to get us there. If we don't respond to Jesus and follow the path that He gave us, we are left stumbling in the dark. We might find our way (through responding to the grace that God gives us to seek and find Him), but we just don't know for sure. And so, the possibility of salvation for those outside the Church does not do away with our need to evangelize. If God has made a sure path to Himself, why would we not share this path with others? And this is precisely our message — we preach the Gospel in order to share with others the path that leads to life, the path that is Jesus Himself, the way, the truth, and the life (see John 14:6).

"Whatever good or truth is found amongst them is considered by the Church to be a preparation for the Gospel and given by Him who enlightens all men that they may at length have life" (*Lumen Gentium,* 16).

What about the other paths — are they all wrong? Of course not. The

Church teaches that these other paths each have elements of truth, and "the Catholic Church rejects nothing of what is true and holy in these religions" (*Nostra Aetate*, 2). The Church does not say that these other religious paths are completely wrong, with nothing of value. No, the Church recognizes that these other paths contain various rays of truth and goodness. But the Church does say that these elements of truth provide just a glimpse of the *fullness* of truth found in the definitive revelation of Jesus Christ. This isn't the Church trying to set itself up as superior to other religions; instead, the Church is affirming its belief in a God who revealed Himself so that all humanity could know the truth and experience the fullness of life with Him. God wants us to know the truth, and so He has revealed Himself to us, a revelation that comes to its peak in the life and message of Jesus.

CHAPTER 5

ISN'T CHRISTIANITY JUST A HYBRID OF OTHER ANCIENT RELIGIONS?

There was a meme created not too long ago that went viral. It depicted the "historic" origins of false gods and deities throughout history and then attempted to say that Christ's story was nothing more than a hybrid of each of these false gods. It's not surprising that such an image would be shared so freely; the fact that there are people who reject Christianity is undeniable, and one very convenient way of rejecting Gospel truth is to claim that the whole thing was just made up. I mean, if we get rid of Jesus as a real, historical person, Christianity itself ends up going out the window. If we can discredit Christianity and the whole Jesus story as being nothing more than the creation of human beings 2,000 years ago, then it will ultimately have to be thrown into the same category as Greek mythology or *Aesop's Fables*. And this is exactly what some people would like to do. This idea is that some people (how many and who, we're not sure) took bits and pieces from other stories, mythologies, and religions in the ancient world, and stamped Jesus' name on them. By borrowing one piece from here and another from there, they were able to retell the same legends that others had told, but with a new set of characters. And (or so the argument goes) since we reject these other mythologies, we ought to reject Christianity as well.

To give an example of these accusations, one of the common claims revolves around the Egyptian god *Horus* and the Roman god *Mithras*. The stories surrounding the lives of these two ancient gods contain elements similar to the stories surrounding the life of Jesus, and so people claim that the first Christians must have just taken these stories and given them a new face in a man called Jesus. Some of these supposed parallels are: the virgin birth, the gathering of disciples, healing the sick and raising the dead, and even Resurrection.

There are many problems with these correlations. For example, many of these connections tend to be very loosely made, highlighting bits and pieces of stories that as a whole vary greatly from the stories about

Jesus. And even when supposed connections are made, the meaning and significance found in the various stories differ greatly from their significance in relation to Jesus. Finally, and most problematic, much of the information about these supposed connections is based upon undocumented, un-scholarly Internet sites (and we all know that if it's on the Internet, it must be true, right?). When claims like this are made, a reasonable response would be to ask for references from real academic sources — you know, from people with letters after their names. The details of the specific claims and their value have been dealt with by many Catholic apologists, but for now, let's turn directly to the question of Jesus and Christianity's claims about Him.

The questions related to the person of Jesus can be boiled down to three basic issues:

(1) Was Jesus a real historical figure?
(2) If so, then who was He?
(3) Were His Resurrection and the miraculous events surrounding His life just a fabrication of the early Christians?

WAS JESUS A REAL HISTORICAL FIGURE?

The great majority of serious historians (Christian or not) admit that what developed into the religion we now call Christianity is based on a historical figure, Jesus of Nazareth. Even if some reject Christianity's claims about Him, they nonetheless admit that these claims are about a real person who actually existed in human history. This is true even if we go all the way back to the first century: Jewish historian Flavius Josephus and Roman historian Cornelius Tacitus (neither of whom were eager to support the claims of Christianity) wrote about Jesus of Nazareth as a real, historical figure. And the view that a man named Jesus actually existed in the first century AD is nearly universally held by modern scholars, many of who are self-proclaimed atheists.

> The great majority of serious historians (Christian or not) admit that what developed into the religion we now call Christianity is based on a historical figure, Jesus of Nazareth.

WHO WAS HE?

Obviously, the mere fact that people believe Jesus really existed in no way proves that what Christians believe about Him is actually true. To answer this question, we need to do what we can to examine His life and ministry and determine what it tells us about Him. Now, many people do not accept the four Gospels as reliable historical documents. And to an extent, it would be correct not to classify them as history in our modern sense of the word. Why? Because they do not contain to-the-minute accounts of Jesus' life as it was happening. It's not as though Matthew was following the "breaking Jesus story" as a modern reporter would follow some world leader or global event.

However, just because the Gospels might not be classified as historical in our contemporary sense, this doesn't mean that they don't contain historically accurate information about Jesus. The Gospel writers never intended to document Jesus' life that way. Instead, they wanted to give us a picture of who Jesus was, what He was about, and why He was here. In doing this, they used real events from Jesus' life and recounted real sayings from Jesus' lips. It was obviously not possible to document every detail of everything Jesus said and did. St. John says in his Gospel that if this were to have been done, the entire world could not contain the books that could be written (see John 21:25). The Gospel writers drew upon the life and ministry of Jesus and presented it to us in a way that revealed who He was, why He came, and how His life and teachings unfolded. And so, in this sense, we can say that the Gospels accurately reflect who Jesus is.

Even if some are skeptical about the details recorded in the Gospels, if we step back we can see at least this much: A man named Jesus went around Palestine in the first century AD; groups of people followed Him; He was reported to have performed miracles; and He taught that He provided unique access to God, even going so far as saying that "the Father and I are one" (John 10:30).

This last point deserves a closer look. Jesus made some pretty wild claims; for one, He claimed He was God. Consider just a few passages as examples:

- "No one knows the Son except the Father, and no one knows the Father except the Son and any one to whom the Son wishes to reveal Him" (Matthew 11:27).

- "He who does not honor the Son does not honor the Father who sent Him" (John 5:23).

- "If you knew Me, you would know my Father also" (John 8:19).

- "He who sees Me sees Him who sent Me" (John 12:45).

In addition to these statements, Jesus also did things that, for His Jewish audience, could only be done by God, such as forgiving sins (see Luke 5:17–26). Both in His words and actions, we see Jesus making claims about Himself that ordinary people don't normally make.

When we consider these claims, we are left with this question: Are they true? Let's imagine that they are not. Where would that leave us? Well, a lot of people these days want to say, "Yeah, I accept Jesus as a prophet, or as a good moral teacher, but I can't believe that He is God." But if we think about it, Jesus being *just* a good moral teacher is really not a reasonable option. I mean, imagine a friend of yours said, "Hey, Sam, I just wanted to let you know that if you want to see God, you need to come to Him through me. And if you reject me, you are ultimately rejecting God, because to see me is to see God." If your friend were to say this to you, you would probably think he or she had gone crazy (or was full of it). Well, the same is true of Jesus.

In making these claims, there are only three options available to us:

1. Jesus was crazy (thinking these things were true but in fact being very delusional).
2. He was purposely trying to deceive us (He knew that they weren't true but wanted us to believe them anyway).
3. What He said was true (He really was who He said He was — the unique way to know and see God).

If what Jesus claimed about Himself were not true, He would either have to be crazy or deceitful, and neither of these would classify Him as a good moral teacher. And so we have to ask ourselves what is most reasonable for us to believe: that Jesus was crazy, that He was a liar, or that He was actually who He said He was — the Son of God? (For a more sophisticated presentation of this idea check out the book *Mere Christianity* by C.S. Lewis.)

WHAT ABOUT THE MIRACLES RECORDED IN THE GOSPELS?

The topic of miracles will be covered more in Chapter 10, but for now, let's look at the biggest one of all, the Resurrection. This claim really stands out as the foundation of Christianity; if it were to be disproved, the whole system would collapse. By the way, St. Paul himself realized this:

> "If Christ has not been raised, your faith is futile [...] If for this life only we have hoped in Christ, we are of all men most to be pitied" (1 Corinthians 15:17,19).

"If Christ has not been raised, your faith is futile" (1 Corinthians 15:17).

So let's consider the Resurrection. Let's suppose for a minute that Jesus *didn't* rise from the dead. One of the common explanations given by those who deny the Resurrection is that the apostles must have stolen Jesus' body and hid it or disposed of it in some way. Now, we know that soon after Jesus' death and supposed Resurrection (remember, we're pretending it didn't happen), the apostles went around telling people that Jesus had indeed risen from the dead and that He had appeared to them. Now, keep in mind that if Jesus didn't really rise from the dead, the apostles would have *known* for sure that He hadn't (because, again, in this scenario they would have been the ones who stole His body), but they still went around telling others that Jesus had risen from the dead. Hmmm...

So far this seems like a plausible situation. It's certainly possible that the apostles could have stolen Jesus' body and made up the whole Resurrection thing. However, it would seem odd to have a group make up a story like this and then go on to establish a religion with such a high standard of morality, included truth-telling. But let's continue... So, word started to get out that there was this group of people who were going around the city telling people that Jesus had risen from the dead, and they were trying to get other people to believe in this risen Jesus. When the Roman authorities heard about this, they got pretty mad because they wanted people to continue to be loyal to the Roman emperor (who they viewed as a god) and continue to participate in their sacrifices (which were signs of the people's loyalty). So the Roman officials started rounding up anyone who was talking about Jesus and asking them if they believed that Jesus rose from the dead. If they said no, the Roman officials would make them offer sacrifices to the Romans gods and let them go; but if they said yes, they were killed.

Many people did, in fact, die for their belief in the Resurrection, and this should not be taken lightly. Some would say these martyrs were just misled — they *believed* that Jesus rose from the dead, but they were wrong. Dying for something one believes to be true but is actually false doesn't prove anything. Fair enough. But eventually the apostles themselves were brought to the Roman officials and given a chance to take back their belief in Jesus' Resurrection and therefore have their lives spared. But ten of the twelve apostles gave up their lives for their belief in Jesus' Resurrection (Judas Iscariot hung himself after he betrayed Jesus, and John was imprisoned because of his belief in Christ but died a natural death).

If the apostles *knew for certain* that Jesus had not risen from the dead (which they would have if they had stolen His body), why would they be willing to die for their supposed belief that He had? No one dies for something they *know* to be a lie when they have absolutely nothing to gain from it. While you might try to say that many people have died for something they believed to be true but were wrong, you couldn't say this about the apostles. They would have known for sure that it wasn't true. And yet they were willing to die; this is a historical fact.

> No one just dies for something that they know to be a lie when they have absolutely nothing to gain from it.

So, what do we make of all this? Well, another explanation for the fact that all the apostles (not to mention the hundreds of other Christians that were put to death) were willing to die for their faith in the Resurrection is that they knew that it was true and believed that their eternal life with God was more important than preserving their earthly life. And so we must decide if it is more reasonable to believe that the apostles were willing to sacrifice their lives for something they knew to be a lie (assuming that they had stolen His body), or that they were willing to give up their lives because they actually saw the truly risen Lord after His death on the cross. This is what sets Jesus apart from Horus or Mithras or any other ancient god. He was a real historical figure, who really claimed to be the Son of God, and who proved it by His Resurrection (for more on the historical authenticity of the Resurrection, check out Question 6 in the book *Truth be Told: Basics in Catholic Apologetics* by Mark Hart and Joe Cady).

CHAPTER 6

THE CHURCH IS ALL ABOUT RULES AND WHAT I CAN'T DO.

Wouldn't life be easier without rules? Just imagine a world with no stoplights or traffic signs or lane markers. Wouldn't this make driving more fun? What right does the city have to take away our freedom to drive as we choose?

Many people view the commandments and rules of the Church this way, as infringing upon our freedom to do as we please. And since all the things that the Church says we can't do seem to be all the really enjoyable things in life, they conclude that the Catholic Church must ultimately just be out to spoil everyone's fun. Take, for example, all the Church's rules about sex: no sex before marriage, no pornography, no adultery, and no masturbation... It's obvious the Church doesn't want anyone to experience the pleasure of sex, right? *Wrong!* Sadly, however, many people think that the Church says no to everything that is fun and pleasurable. As a result of this view, they reject the Church and all of her "thou shall nots." What's even worse, there are many in the Church, faithful people who identify themselves as Catholics and believers in God, who have a similar view of the commandments of God. While they might try to follow the rules and commandments of God as taught by the Church, they still view them as ultimately restricting rather than freeing.

Let me give you an example. Have you ever heard someone say, "This is so good that it should be sinful"? The idea behind what they are saying is that because this is so good, enjoyable, or pleasurable, it should be considered as sin. But what does this actually mean? Most likely the person saying this doesn't actually think this thing (usually a delicious dessert) is sinful. But it does reveal an interesting assumption: All the things that God and the Church usually call "sins" are things that are good, enjoyable, or pleasurable, so in forbidding sins, God and the Church are ultimately trying to keep us from the really enjoyable things in life.

Not only is this entirely false, this understanding of God's "thou shall nots" is actually itself at the root of those things that the Church does in fact call sin.

DISOBEDIENCE = LACK OF TRUST IN GOD'S GOODNESS

The idea that God's commandments are meant to keep us from what is good and what will make us happy is the very belief that leads us to sin in the first place. At the root of sin is the belief that God's commands exist for our harm rather than for our good. For example, in the Book of Genesis, there is an account of the creation of our first parents and the beginnings of humanity's relationship with God. In the second creation account (there are two accounts of creation in Genesis, each teaching us unique truths about God, ourselves, and our relationship with Him), God creates a man out of the dust of the ground, and after putting him into a deep sleep, creates a woman out of one of the man's ribs (for the full account, read Genesis 2:4–25). The man and woman are then placed in a garden, full of trees, plants, and animals. They are given only one command: to not eat from one particular tree in the garden: the Tree of Knowledge of Good and Evil. God said, "From that tree you shall not eat; when you eat from it you will die" (Genesis 2:17).

There is a lot that could be said about the meaning and significance of this account of creation (to learn more, check out *CCC* 369–379), but what is important for our purposes is what happens next. Now, it's important to keep in mind that when God first created Adam and Eve, He created them *rightly ordered*. This means that their relationship with God, with each other, and with all creation was marked by harmony; there was no sin, no suffering, and no death. You see, God created our first parents so they could experience the very life and goodness of God, and this communion of life and love was meant to be shared with and experienced by each and every person throughout history. But something very tragic happened at the beginning of creation — disobedience entered human history, and with it death and a rupture of our communion with God and each other.

"God created all things not to increase His glory, but to show it forth and communicate it, for God has no other reason for creating than His love and goodness" (*CCC* 293).

How did this occur? Well, in Genesis 3:1–24, we read about a confrontation between our first parents and a serpent (which has traditionally been identified by the Church as the devil). Adam and Eve had all they needed, because God had placed them in a garden of abundance, free from sin, suffering, and death. They were in communion and harmony with God and each other. God's only instruction was that they not eat from the Tree of Knowledge of Good and Evil. But when the serpent came along, he began to question everything that Adam and Eve had received. Not only that, but he began to question the very goodness of God as a loving Father.

He asked Eve, "Did God really tell you not to eat from any of the trees in the garden?" (Genesis 3:1). Eve tells the serpent that they are free to eat from all the trees in the garden except for the one in the middle of the garden, and that God told them that the moment they eat of it they will die. In response, the serpent says, "You certainly will not die. No, God knows well that the moment you eat of it your eyes will be opened, and you will be like gods, knowing what is good and what is bad" (Genesis 3:5). Now, the Bible doesn't exactly say this, but you can almost hear the serpent say, "Oh, you mean God told you not to eat from that one, the *best tree in the whole garden*? You know, that is just like God; of course He doesn't want you to eat that one. That tree is awesome, and if you eat from it you're going to become just like Him." Now, again, none of that is directly said in Scripture, but look at what the Bible *does* say next, Eve "saw that the tree was good for food and pleasing to the eyes, and the tree was desirable for gaining wisdom" (Genesis 3:6). At that moment it seems likely that Eve began to think to herself, *this is a good tree, why doesn't God want me to eat from it?* And with that, doubt entered into her heart.

You see, the whole idea here is that the serpent is leading Adam and Eve to question God. Rather than trusting in God as their loving Father who wants to give them only what is good and beautiful, the serpent wants them to see God as an enemy who is keeping them from the really good things in life. It's the same with us. When we begin to view God's commands as being for our harm rather than for our good, we open the door to sin. When we trust someone, we naturally want to follow what that person tells us.

For example, when you trust that your soccer coach wants you to be in good shape and have the endurance needed to play well, you're most likely going to have no problem listening to him when he tells you to begin each practice by running a mile. However, if you think your coach is just trying to give you

"Man, tempted by the devil, let his trust in his Creator die in his heart and, abusing his freedom, disobeyed God's command" (*CCC* 397).

extra work because he thinks you're lazy, you probably would be less inclined to listen to him. In the same way, we will be more inclined to follow God if we trust that He knows best and gives us commands

> "All subsequent sin would be disobedience toward God and lack of trust in His goodness" (*CCC* 397).

because He loves us and wants us to be free from things that will hurt us. However, the moment we begin to think that God doesn't actually want what is best for us, our trust in Him fades, and our willingness to disobey Him increases. In fact, the *Catechism* teaches that this lack of trust in God is at the root of all subsequent sin. In a certain sense, every act of disobedience is a manifestation of lack of trust in God as a loving Father who wants us to be happy.

Now, in light of all this, let's go back and reconsider the idea that the rules and commandments of God and the Church exist to keep us from what is good and pleasurable.

SEEKING HAPPINESS = SEEKING GOD

Ultimately, what all of us want is to be happy. No human being would say, "Nah, I'm not really interested in being happy." But here's the thing: God wants us to be happy, too. That might seem silly to say, or even self-evident, but think about it. *God wants us to be happy.* Not just kind of happy, but fully happy. He doesn't want us to settle for a lesser happiness that He gives in relation to some "greater" happiness found in the world; He wants us to be completely and perfectly happy. You see, our desire for happiness comes from God Himself. God put this desire within us so we would naturally seek Him, the only One who can really and truly make us happy. Our search for happiness is synonymous with our search for God. Another way of saying this is that we will only find happiness to the extent that we find God. It's when we believe that seeking God is somehow opposed to seeking happiness that we throw our entire lives out of whack. When we think that God's commandments exist as a restriction to freedom and a hindrance to happiness, we are missing the whole point.

> "This desire is of divine origin: God has placed it in the human heart in order to draw man to the One who alone can fulfill it" (*CCC* 1718).

God is a loving Father who says, "yes" to human happiness. And any "no" that God may say is ultimately saying "no" to that which is bad for us. When God says, "Thou shall not," what He is ultimately saying is "Don't do this, because this will hurt you; it will prevent you from being truly happy; this is not good for you." God's laws (and, by extension, the "rules" of the Church) are certainly there to keep us from sin, but that is because sin is bad for us. Even when we think that what the Church forbids is keeping us from something that appears good or pleasurable, it is because the Church is trying to enable us to experience goodness or pleasure fully — in a way that really will make us happy.

Consider again the example of sex. The Church doesn't say "no" to sex, but it does say "no" to anything that would prevent us from experiencing the *fullness* of what sex was meant to be. The Church doesn't prohibit premarital sex because sex is bad. The Church forbids premarital sex because it is only in the context of a lifelong, faithful marriage that the goodness of sex will be most fully experienced. The Church has "rules" about sex because sex is *good*. And the Church wants to ensure that we don't settle for anything less that the real deal. (Here's something to blow your mind: St. Thomas Aquinas said that Adam and Eve would have experienced more pleasure in sex before the fall than after because it would have been free of any self-interest — so much for the Church being "down on sex"!) Consider a basketball game: Are the rules there to restrict the players? Of course not. They are there to enable everyone involved to experience basketball to its fullest. The same is true of God's laws; they are given to enable us to experience the fullness of life — a life *free* from what brings harm and disorder, a life *full* of love and happiness.

Ultimately, if we view the Church's rules and commandments as restrictive, we will inevitably break them. Why? Because we want what is good (or what we think is good), and if we think that God's laws are hindering our ability to have those things, then we pridefully and selfishly will set those laws aside. Why, for example, do kids disobey the rules that their parents set for them? Because they think that by doing so they are actually going to get some good thing that the rules are keeping them from. ("But Mom, you just have to let me stay out past midnight — this party is going to be so fun; everyone is going to be there!") But most of the time, what we think is good is only a partial or lesser good. God wants the most good for us. God wants us to be happy (even more than we want to be happy ourselves). And it is only when we combine (in our minds and hearts) our quest for happiness with a quest for God that we will ever truly be happy. Only when we realize that God's "no" to this or that is part of an overall "yes" to what we really want (perfect happiness) will we begin to trust God as the loving Father that He is.

So the question isn't really whether rules are good or bad for us — they *are* good. The real question is whether or not we trust the Rule-giver.

CHAPTER 7

HOW CAN I BE PART OF A CHURCH WITH SUCH A TAINTED HISTORY?

Weren't the Crusades an attempt by the Church to force people to either convert to Catholicism or die? Didn't the Church put to death thousands of people during the Inquisition just because they didn't agree with Catholic teaching? You may have heard these claims before or others like them. They are commonly brought up as attempts to discredit the Church. The idea behind them is that if the Church *really* exists as a part of God's will (as the Church claims), how could its history be filled with such terrible things? There are other claims made as well, but the Crusades and the Inquisition tend to be the ones that pop up most frequently.

The way the story of the Crusades normally goes is that Christians went throughout Europe with a simple message: Convert and believe in Christianity or be killed. What is usually left out of the story is that these religious crusades were undertaken to reclaim lands that were previously Christian and which had been conquered by Muslim forces as Islam expanded. The Crusades were not motivated by the intention to convert the whole world by force; they were attempts to reclaim land that for centuries had been a part of Christendom (including the Holy Land).

Regarding the Inquisition, it is commonly assumed that the Church went on a hunt far and wide for anyone remotely deviating from the Church's standard of orthodoxy and, once found, subjected these individuals to torture and ultimately death. What you won't usually hear is that the courts of the Inquisition were considered so just and fair in comparison to other courts of the day that many people preferred to have their case heard before the inquisitors rather than these other courts. Another thing that typically is left out of the story is the fact that recent research related to the history of the Inquisition and the Crusades reveals that a lot of what is generally accepted as fact has little actual basis in history.[1]

---

1   For a good overview of these events, check out the CD series from St. Joseph Communications called *Fire and Sword*.

Now, none of this minimizes or excuses any of the unacceptable things that occurred during this period of the Church's history, but when it comes to discrediting an entire religion or institution because of its history, it is important to make sure that we have the story right. And what recent historical research is telling us is that there is more to the story than what we are usually told.

WHAT ABOUT CORRUPTION IN OUR OWN TIME?

Most people today are not so concerned with these events from the distant past. The most problematic issue surrounding the Catholic Church for people today is most likely the sexual abuse scandal in the United States and throughout the world. Please understand, nothing that is said here should be understood as minimizing or taking lightly the reality that people have been victims of abuse from those in leadership within the Catholic Church. Such abuse is unacceptable because it is an offense against the dignity of those who have been abused and a violation of the trust and confidence that people should be able to place in their religious leaders. We must pray always that those who have been victims of abuse might experience the healing love of God and the fullness of communion that the Church offers.

In addition to the psychological and emotional effects it has on its victims, sexual abuse can often have damaging effects upon the personal faith of the victims, their families, and those close to them. And it doesn't stop there. The sexual abuse scandal has had the further effect of shaking the faith of numerous Catholics who were not themselves directly affected by the abuse, as well as causing many outside the Church to no longer even consider Catholicism as a realistic option for themselves. Whether we like it or not, this is a reality that we have to deal with. You see, the fact of the matter is that the world judges the Catholic Church by what it sees in the lives and actions of individual Catholics. For better or for worse, people form an image of what Catholicism is all about by the example set by the Catholics they know.

TRUTH VS. CREDIBILITY

It is important to make a clarification here. The *actual* Truth of the Gospel (Truth with a capital "T") or the teachings of the Catholic Church is in no way connected to the extent to which that truth is or is not lived out in the lives of Christians. If something is true, it is *true*, period! For example, the statement "Jesus is the Way, the Truth, and the Life. No one comes to the Father except through Me" (John 14:6) is true even if only 5 percent of those who call themselves Christians actually believe this or live their lives accordingly. It's not true because people believe it; people believe it because it is true. That being said, the *credibility* of this statement before others *is* connected to the witness of those who claim to be Christians.

Let's say you know fifty Christians. How likely would you be to accept the statement "Jesus is Lord" if only one of these fifty Christians believed this statement and lived accordingly? Probably not that likely. To put it in the context of another "hot button" issue, how much more credibility would the Church's stance against artificial contraception have if the majority of Catholics actually accepted this and lived according to it? The *truth* of the Church's teaching on contraception is not determined by the beliefs or practices of particular Catholics (contrary to what some might say), but the *credibility* of this teaching can be greatly damaged by a lack of fidelity on the part of those who identify themselves as Catholic. To put it simply, the truth of Christianity is not tied to the life and behavior of individual Christians, *but its credibility in the world is!* And it is for this reason that, in addition to the tragic harm done to its victims, the sexual abuse scandal has been damaging to the Church's image and credibility in the world as a whole.

In light of all this, how do we respond to those who say they could never be Catholic after all the abuse that has been done by its leaders?

First, we should not deny that such abuse has in fact happened; without honesty we will never be able to move in the right direction. Secondly, we should remind them (and ourselves) that even though the Church is built upon the truth of Jesus Christ and the power of the Holy Spirit, it is also made up of fallen, sinful human beings; the Church, like Christ, is both *human and divine*. Unfortunately, there will be times when others (even Church leaders we trust) will let us down and fall short of the standard to which they are called. All Christians, from the pope to the parishioners sitting next to us at Mass, are sinners. Now, this is not an excuse for sin, but it is an explanation for it. This is why, no matter how much we might like a particular priest, sister, teacher, or anyone else we look up to in the Church, our faith and our eyes should always be fixed on Jesus first, as the "leader and perfecter of faith" (Hebrews 12:2).

Lastly, we must remember that what makes the teachings of the Catholic Church true is not the holiness of its members but the trustworthiness of the One who revealed these things to us, Jesus Christ, the eternal Son of God, who came to set us free with the truth that He gives (John 8:32). The failures of particular priests (though tragic and harmful) do not change the truth of Catholicism. It doesn't change the fact that through Baptism we are reborn as children of God, or that through Confirmation we are empowered by the Holy Spirit to grow in holiness and virtue and so experience life and love as God intends, or that in the Eucharist we receive the very body and blood, soul and divinity of Christ as food that endures to eternal life. Even in the darkest times in the Church's history, the truth and goodness of God's revelation has remained constant. It is in this Truth, not its teachers, that we place our confidence and trust. The good news is that God's holiness is infinitely greater than our sinfulness. And the truth of the Gospel is stronger than our weakness in following it.

The Church's history is not spotless. And the credibility of the Church is, for better or for worse, intimately connected to the example that Catholics set in the world. This is why it is so important that we seek always to live according to the new life we have received in Christ — always seeking to grow in virtue, self-giving love, humility, and repentance when we sin so that, hopefully, with the help of God's grace, people might see our faith and love and be moved to love God who is the source of these things in us.

"Your light must shine before others, that they may see your good deeds and glorify your heavenly Father" (Matthew 5:16).

The fact is, we might be the only image of the Church that people ever see. Therefore, we should live as though we were constantly wearing a shirt that says "Hold me accountable to the Gospel." How different would our days look if this were the case? Let us pray that, as people meet us, they will encounter Christ in us.

CHAPTER 8
RELIGION IS JUST A CRUTCH FOR THE WEAK AND UNEDUCATED.

Most of us have heard of the Dark Ages, but very few of us seem to know when they occurred or even why they are called that. The story goes like this: After the dawn of philosophy (with people like Socrates, Plato, and Aristotle), there was a long period of time when reason was stifled by the "oppressive rule of religion" (specifically, the supposedly "anti-reason," "anti-science" Catholic Church). This "bondage" of the human mind was not overcome until the golden age of reason and science that history now calls the Enlightenment. What made the Dark Ages *dark* was the absence of those things that enlighten the mind — namely, human reason and science. But there's more to the story: In the Dark Ages most people were uneducated, and so in a certain sense they *needed* an institution like the Catholic Church to maintain order in society. But now, with the development of science, mathematics, and philosophical reasoning, the Church and religious faith have become almost obsolete. Any value that religion and faith may have had in the past (in those Dark Ages) is now, with the triumph of reason over faith, completely unnecessary; no "smart" person has any need for them.

The question of how faith and reason are related to each other will be covered in the next chapter. But for now, let's take a look at the idea that religion is only for the uneducated and weak. At the heart of this view is the assumption that "religious people" or "believers" either are not intelligent enough to think for themselves or are so emotionally fragile that they need to believe in something external in order to give their lives meaning and direction. Regarding the first assumption, I'd like to see someone say that to St. Thomas Aquinas. Of course, he is a saint who was both loving and humble, and he would not be interested in an intellectual showdown, but the fact remains that I would take him against anyone in a battle of human reason. He is recognized, even by those outside of Christianity, as one of the greatest minds western civilization has seen. The claim that people of faith are universally ignorant or that religion is only for the uneducated is simply nonsense.

Just look at the brilliant minds of people like John Paul II or Benedict XVI. They were not "uneducated" by any stretch, and yet when we look at their lives we see immense faith and trust in God.

OUR NATURAL DESIRE FOR GOD

What about the second idea that religion is just for the weak? Well, we must ask ourselves, is it that these people "need" something to believe in, or is it that they recognize that there must be more to life than what we can see here and now? Are these people responding to an inherent weakness in themselves, or do they recognize the fact that they are only a small piece of a much larger reality? Is it possible that these people who "need" to believe in something are responding to something real inside of them? If so, what could this something be? Well, the Church calls it a *natural desire for God*. You see, God made us for love, to love and be loved, and so experience what He is in His very essence, a communion of love.

The ultimate purpose for our lives can only be found in the One for whom we were made. God created us with an intellect, a will, and an immortal soul so that we might *know* Him, *love* Him, and *live forever* with Him. These gifts (intellect, will, and soul) were given to us for the sake of using them to be in relationship with Him, and so they are only fully used when we *know* the truth, *love* as God loves, and *live eternally* in the Kingdom of heaven. We have a natural desire for God because we came from God and are destined to return to Him. So when people manifest a "need" for God, they are not creating some arbitrary thing to make them happy, they are responding to a real inner longing to know, love, and live with the God who made them.

Ultimately, what it comes down to is a question of what religion is for in the first place. Many think that religion is just something created by people to meet some emotional or psychological need. But in reality, religion is something that seeks to help us achieve the very reason for our existence. Religion is our way of giving concrete form to our natural desire for God. Why is it that every culture has had some sort of religious expression to orient their lives? It's because people, in various ways, have always sought to respond to this natural desire for God. And in doing so, they have created rituals and ethical codes that orient their lives according to a particular worldview. This isn't the mark of weakness (at least in the sense meant by critics of religion); it is the mark of people recognizing their smallness in relation to the Universe and their attempt to give expression to it. Put simply, religion doesn't seek to proclaim how great humanity is but instead recognizes that we are *not* the center of the universe.

These expressions have varied from culture to culture throughout history, but what they have in common is being rooted in humanity's natural desire for God. This is why God revealed Himself — He wanted to provide us with a way of achieving the very reason for our existence, to know and love God as He truly is. And while God's grace is able to draw people to Himself through these various religious expressions (as we saw in chapter 4), it is ultimately Jesus Christ who provides an answer to humanity's search for God. Through Christ, God reached into the world in order raise us up to Himself and give us a share in His own life.

"All religions bear witness to men's essential search for God" (*CCC* 2566).

Let's look again at the idea that religion only had value (if it ever *did* have value) in the Dark Ages, when people didn't know what we know today. Remember, the basic idea here is that now that we have access to science, technology, and philosophy we really don't need religion. There is one problem, though: None of these things have been able to satisfy our natural desire for God. None of these things have brought us the ultimate fulfillment that we seek. Scientific discovery, technological advancement, and philosophical sophistication (all of which the Church values greatly) cannot ultimately bring us the happiness we desire, because that happiness is found only in knowing and loving God.

TRUE HUMAN PROGRESS

The Church is not opposed to philosophy, science, or technology; in fact, the Church is seriously interested in these things. (Did you know that there is a Pontifical Academy of Science, whose mission is "to promote the progress of the mathematical, physical, and natural sciences, and the study of epistemological problems relating thereto"? Not bad for a religion accused of being opposed to scientific progress.) The Church holds human reason in very high esteem, but it does not accept the idea that its progress leads to the abandonment of religious faith (more on this in the next chapter).

The basic attitude of the Enlightenment toward religion was that religious faith somehow made human beings less.. The Church, however, holds the exact opposite view. Faith, which gives us access to a relationship with the very One for whom and by whom we were made, is precisely part of what it means to be human. This is why the Second Vatican Council said that atheism was "one of the most serious problems of our time" (*Gaudium et Spes*, 19). Therefore, what the Church proposes for the world is not a hindrance to humanity's progress; instead, it serves to facilitate it. But progress only makes sense when we understand what we are progressing *toward*. The Church provides the answer: We are moving toward our ultimate fulfillment in God, a God who is known here by faith.

So, is religion for the weak? You tell me. Consider the truly heroic virtue of some of our more modern saints — Maria Goretti, Maximilian Kolbe, and Mother Teresa. Through their unfailing commitment to selfless love, they show us that faith is not a tool used by the weak to give them comfort and consolation. Faith is a source of divine life that empowers us to love in life-changing ways. Their faith was not a manifestation of some emotional, psychological, or intellectual shortcoming; it was the manifestation of an intense realization that God is love and that the purpose of life is to conform ourselves to that very same love. Through the saints and martyrs of the Church, we get a glimpse of what true strength looks like. Faith isn't for the weak and uneducated; it is for all of us, so that by it we might come to know and love God in this life and to see Him fully in the next.

> "The dignity of man rests above all on the fact that he is called to communion with God [...] For if man exists it is because God has created him through love, and through love continues to hold him in existence. He cannot live fully according to truth unless he freely acknowledges that love and entrusts himself to his creator" (*Gaudium et Spes,* 19).

> "Faith makes us taste in advance the light of the beatific vision, the goal of our journey here below" (*CCC* 163).

CHAPTER 9

CHRISTIANS JUST BLINDLY BELIEVE; I WANT TO KNOW THE TRUTH, WHICH IS WHY I CAN'T BE A CHRISTIAN.

Many people basically assume that *believing* is somehow opposed to *knowing* and that therefore Christianity is ultimately a hindrance to true knowledge. According to this perspective, Christianity is nothing more than a blind, un-informed acceptance of unverifiable claims, while science and human reason are based on evidence and logic. A line is drawn that divides science (reason) and religion (faith). Real knowledge (so it is claimed) can only come from the scientific side of things, while religion and faith (although comforting or inspiring) don't actually provide us with any reliable knowledge and so shouldn't really be taken seriously when it comes to knowing what is true.

Ultimately the key issue here is knowledge: What can we know, and how can we know it? The Catholic Church, contrary to what people think, is very interested in knowledge of the truth. Jesus Himself said, "You will know the truth, and the truth will set you free" (John 8:32). St. Thomas Aquinas said that truth is the "ultimate end of the whole Universe" (*Summa Contra Gentiles*, 2). Pope Emeritus Benedict XVI said that the Church "searches for truth, proclaims it tirelessly and recognizes it wherever it is manifested" (*Caritas in Veritate*, 9). The point here is that truth holds a central place in the life and mission of the Church. Any claim that the Church is trying to keep people in the dark or prevent people from growing in knowledge must be rejected as utterly ridiculous.

"The desire for truth is part of human nature itself" (*Fides et Ratio*, 3).

The Church should never be considered in any way opposed to science, philosophy, or reason. The Church places great value on the ability of human reason to arrive at truth and make known to us many valuable things. But this ability is not absolute. The human mind is incredibly powerful, but its power is limited. While there is much that we can and do know through reason, there are also many things that are simply beyond our reach. Many modern "intellectuals," however, fall into the trap of overestimating the potential of human reason. This tendency has its roots in the rationalism of the 18th and 19th centuries, which claimed that human reason was sufficient to know all there was to know. Nothing else was needed — not divine revelation, not religious indoctrination, and certainly not faith.

While there is nothing wrong with valuing human reason and its abilities, it becomes problematic when we begin to think that human reason is all we need or that it is entirely sufficient to know all there is to know. You see, the Church recognizes that there is another form of knowledge, another way of knowing truth: through *faith*. In fact, there are some things that can *only* be known through faith (such as the understanding of God as the Trinity). Therefore, it's important to realize that truth can be known either by the *light of reason* or by the *light of faith*. We call these ways of knowing truth "lights" because they are ways in which truth is seen or illuminated.

The Church teaches that truth can be found through faith *or* through reason. But — and here's the really important part — *these "truths" cannot be opposed to each other*. Truth is truth, period. There is not one truth that comes through reason and another that comes through faith — there is just truth. Even though there are different paths to arrive there, there is only one destination.

This is an important distinction, because there are some who say that reason and faith (or science and religion) contradict each other. And therefore, if someone is serious about truth and the findings of modern science, they must abandon faith and religion. Sadly this view is quite common... and quite wrong. It's based on the mistaken belief that faith and reason are incompatible and ultimately opposed to one another. Faith, however, does not oppose reason; faith exceeds reason (more on this in chapter 12). In reality, there can *never* be any real contradiction between faith and reason. If there *appears* to be a contradiction, either what you believe by faith is wrong, or the conclusions you've come to through reason are incorrect. Remember, there is only one truth, and God is the ultimate source of that truth. This means that when scientific research seeks to grow in its knowledge of the Universe, these findings can never contradict a truth of the faith.

"Since the same God who reveals mysteries and infuses faith has bestowed the light of reason on the human mind, God cannot deny Himself, nor can truth ever contradict truth" (*CCC* 159).

THE DANGER OF FALSE CONTRADICTIONS

When people try to set up some sort of opposition or contradiction between what science (or reason) tells us and what faith tells us, they are creating a conflict that isn't actually there. One of the most common examples of this is the argument between creationism and evolution. People look at the first chapters of Genesis (which speak of God creating the world in six days) and say that the findings of modern science clearly show that the Bible is wrong. The first problem with this line of reasoning is that these people take the words of Genesis far too literally. While there are some Christians who do read Genesis 1 in this way, the Catholic Church has never taught that the Book of Genesis teaches scientific facts about *how* the world came into being. No, the allegorical accounts of creation in Genesis were written to teach *theological truth*: truths about God, about ourselves, and about our relationship with Him and all creation. Therefore, it doesn't really matter what science discovers about the origin of the world; these findings have very little to do with what is written in Genesis. In fact, the Church encourages scientists to explore creation and discover all they can about how the world came into being.

With regard to evolution, the Church is open to the *possibility* that human life developed in stages over time through a process of evolution. There is one catch, however. Any theory about the origins of humanity must acknowledge two important truths: (1) that God is the ultimate source and author of life — nothing came to be without His instigation and involvement; and (2) that the human soul comes into being by a direct, creative act of God. Being open to a variety of scientific explanations about *how* or *when* the world came into being does not require us to abandon what the Bible tells us about *why* the world was made.

"It is not only a question of knowing when and how the universe arose physically, or when man appeared, but rather of discovering the meaning of such an origin" (*CCC* 284).

The truth that comes through science and human reason provides a valuable contribution to our overall knowledge of the world, but it does not tell us the entire story. Discovering *how* we got here does not provide answers to the questions of *why* we are here or *where* we are going. These are the kinds of questions answered though divine revelation. By divine revelation we mean all that God has revealed to the world (through people like Abraham, Moses, the prophets, and ultimately Jesus) about who He is, why He made us, and how we are called to live in relation to Him and each other. It is only when God reveals Himself to us that we are able to know the truth about the meaning and purpose of creation.

"Men and women are always called to direct their steps toward a truth which transcends them" (*Fides et Ratio,* 5).

ONE TRUTH

Here's a good way to keep all of this straight: Faith and reason do not provide us with different truths but with different paths to *the* truth. In fact, while there are some things reason simply could never tell us (such as the fact that God is a Trinity, or Jesus' nature being fully human and fully divine), many of the things that faith reveals to us are things that we *could* know independently of religion. For example, in the Ten Commandments God says, "You shall not kill" (Exodus 20:13). Therefore, we *know* that murder is wrong. Why? Because God has *revealed* to us that taking the life of another is not good for humanity. But this is not something that you need to be Christian (or any other religion) to know. By reason alone we can know that taking the life of another is wrong — that it is bad for humans to kill one another. We discover this truth simply by looking at the nature of what it means to be a living person. Through reason we recognize that life is better for humanity than death. There are many things like this that we are able to know by human reason alone (in fact, three out of five of the books that make up St. Thomas Aquinas' great work, *Summa Contra Gentiles,* refer to things that we can know by reason apart from divine revelation).

However, if we can know these things by reason, why does God also reveal them to us? If we can know by reason that we ought not to kill each other, why did God tell us, "You shall not kill"?

The answer is simple: We are dense.

SIN IS DARKNESS

You see, because of sin our very nature has been wounded. Our minds have become darkened and our wills have been weakened. It doesn't take long to realize this. So often we choose to do things that seem good for us but turn out to actually be bad for us (eating an entire box of donuts for breakfast *seems* great, but do this for a few months and tell me how it goes). The fact is, our minds are a bit out of whack, and so we have trouble distinguishing good from bad, truth from error. Therefore, God chose to include in divine revelation even those things that we can know through reason so that we could know them with *certainty*.

There are many things that can get in the way of our coming to know the truth (busyness, lack of education, laziness, the difficulties of life, etc.). And even when we do discover the truth about something, oftentimes that truth is mixed with a bunch of non-truths or partial truths. Therefore, God chose to reveal to us everything that we needed to know so that everyone could have easy access to this truth. And, in fact, the knowledge that comes through faith in what God has revealed is more trustworthy than

"In the present situation sinful man needs grace and revelation so moral and religious truths may be known by everyone with facility, with firm certainty and with no admixture of error" (*CCC* 1960).

the knowledge that comes through reason. That may sound kind of crazy, but think about it. When God reveals something as true, we can stand upon that truth with absolute certainty, not because we can verify it through our reason (remember, we often draw wrong conclusions about what is and is not true), but because we trust is God the Revealer.

"Methodological research in all branches of knowledge, provided it is carried out in a truly scientific manner and does not override moral laws, can never conflict with the Faith, because the things of the world and the things of faith derive from the same God" (*CCC* 159).

We trust in divine revelation because of the trustworthiness of the One who reveals it to us — God, who *is* truth. There is an old prayer, the Act of Faith, which ends with the phrase, "I believe these and all the truths which the holy Catholic Church teaches, because You have revealed them, who can neither deceive nor be deceived." Notice that last line: God can *neither deceive nor be deceived*. This is why we believe what He has revealed, because it is impossible for Him to lie to us.

Since God is so much more trustworthy than our darkened intellects, knowledge through faith in what God reveals is more certain than knowledge through reason. Therefore, if you want to "know" the truth, this should not be a reason to run from the Church. This is what the Church wants as well, and she never ceases to make known to us the truth that has been entrusted to her. Any notion that faith and science (or philosophy, or ethics, or metaphysics) are somehow in conflict with each other is simply, well... *not true*. All truth has its source in God, and in Him there can be no contradiction.

CHAPTER 10
YOU DON'T ACTUALLY BELIEVE IN MIRACLES, DO YOU?

The question of miracles is one that can really trip people up. Many people might be willing to jump on board with some of Christianity's moral teachings, or accept the value of some of the wisdom found in the Bible, but when they start looking at the supposed supernatural events found there, that's where they draw the line. Jesus' so called miracles are pushed aside as nothing more than made-up stories by the Gospel writers to make Jesus seem more credible. For many people, believing in miracles simply seems unbelievable.

The same is true of so-called miracles today. Any claims of miraculous events are generally dismissed as either exaggerated or as having some other natural cause we just haven't discovered yet. Why? Most likely it's because these people don't believe in God, and if you don't believe in God you certainly aren't going to believe in any sort of divine intervention or miraculous event. With the commitment to the view that there is no God comes a commitment to the belief that all events, everything that occurs in life, has some natural cause and explanation.

Obviously the question of God's existence is very relevant here. But let's look a bit closer at miracles themselves and what the Church believes about them. First of all, what exactly is a miracle? The *Catechism* defines a miracle as "a sign or wonder, such as a healing or the control of nature, which can only be attributed to divine power" (*CCC* glossary). Basically, a miracle is an event or occurrence where the *cause* must ultimately be attributed to the direct action of God.

Of course, in a certain sense, everything that occurs in history has God as its ultimate cause, since all creation has its source in God, the Creator. But a miracle is some divine action that is inserted into the normal course of events; it is something that would not have occurred had all natural causes been uninterrupted. You see, God set up the world to function in a certain way, with certain laws (such as gravity and the movement of the planets). And so, when these things proceed as God set them up, this is considered the normal course of events (there is no miracle involved in the sun rising and setting each day). A miracle is an occurrence that takes place *outside* the normal course of events, something which wouldn't have happened without the direct action of God. An example is what happened in Fatima when the Blessed Virgin Mary appeared — the sun appeared to spin around in the sky.

Obviously, if you don't believe in God, you are never going to believe that there are events caused by God's direct intervention. At the same time, the very occurrence of miracles has often been the reason many people come to faith in God in the first place. Therefore, arguing for God's existence from the starting point of miraculous occurrences is not entirely useless. If miracles do happen, there must be a God who is the source and cause of these miraculous events.

MIRACLES STILL HAPPEN

So, we are left with the question: Do miracles happen? The Church responds with a definitive "yes." The entire history of Christianity is filled with accounts of miraculous events that can only be attributed to God as the ultimate cause. Some people have been healed through the prayer and intercession of holy men and women, others have been miraculously protected when attempts were made to put them to death, and still others saw visions and received revelations at various times and places in history. Were the people who experienced these events simply mistaken? Did they make up the stories? Some might say so. They would argue that what seems to be a miracle is nothing more than an extremely unlikely occurrence that has some natural explanation. But making this claim reveals a certain biased perspective. You see, when it comes to so-called miraculous events, those who deny them start with the basic premise that any explanation is possible — *except* the possibility of a miracle.

In his book *The Blind Watchmaker*, Richard Dawkins gives the example of a statue of the Blessed Virgin Mary that appeared to wave.[2] If such an event were to occur, Dawkins said there would have to be some logical, natural cause, such as all the molecules of the statue happening to move by chance at the same time, in the same direction. While the likelihood of this happening is extremely low, it is not technically impossible. For people who would deny miracles (like Richard Dawkins), all explanations are held as possible except one,

---

2   Richard Dawkins, *The Blind Watchmaker: Why the Evidence of Evolution Reveals a Universe without Design* (New York:W. W. Norton & Company, 1996).

the miraculous. But in this case, what seems more plausible, that God intervened directly to miraculously cause the statue to wave, or that the molecules of the statue all moved (by chance) at the same time in the same direction? To deny the believability of a miracle by an even more unbelievable explanation doesn't seem that convincing. The fact of the matter is that things do occur for which the most reasonable explanation is that we can't explain it in natural terms.

> "No event that is more miraculous than the miracle that it seeks to discredit can be used as an explanation to deny that a miracle actually occurred" (Scott Hahn and Benjamin Wiker, *Answering the New Atheism*, 15).

While the Church certainly believes that miracles can and do occur, an important point must be made. The Church does not go around looking for any unlikely occurrence, eager to label it as a miracle. Instead, when claims of a miraculous event are brought forth, the Church looks closely at it, searching for some natural explanation. It is only when no such explanation can be found that the Church opens the door to the possibility of a miracle having occurred. The Church actually determines something to be a miracle as a last possible explanation. So, when someone reports spotting an image of the Blessed Virgin Mary in a piece of toast, the Church's first response isn't, "It's a miracle!" The Church certainly accepts that miracles do happen, but the Church is also very hesitant to throw this label around too loosely.

WAY BACK WHEN...

What about all the so-called miracles in the Bible? The Gospels are filled with accounts of Jesus healing people, expelling demons, and bringing the dead back to life. When reading these accounts we might very naturally ask ourselves, *Did all this really happen?* Underneath this question is a more general question about the reliability of the Gospels as historical documents. As we mentioned before, we can't approach the Gospels from the standpoint of modern historical methods. When Matthew, Mark, Luke, and John sat down to write their Gospels, they did not do so from the standpoint of disinterested news reporters. They approached the Gospels as a literary work. They drew upon Jesus' entire life and ministry and tried to recapture its essence in narrative form. But in doing this they may have combined different elements of Jesus' teaching in a sequence that was different from the chronological order in which they originally occurred. The same is true of Jesus' life. While the accounts of Jesus' ministry in the Gospels are based on the real history of Jesus of Nazareth, it is certainly possible that the Gospel writers arranged those events in different ways in order to emphasize a particular point or aspect of Jesus' life. What this means is that Jesus' life and ministry may not have unfolded exactly as it is presented to us in any one of the Gospels. But this doesn't mean that the Gospels are not historically accurate.

"We may conclude that the Synoptics were intended as an expression of faith and as a basis for faith. But it was a faith founded on historical facts. Hence the Synoptic genre is one that presents facts within a theological framework" (Rev. William G. Most, *The Consciousness of Christ*, 20).

The Gospel writers were far less interested in providing their readers with particular details than they were in presenting their readers with an understanding and overall picture of Jesus. In a certain sense, the Gospels are like pieces of art, utilizing different styles and techniques of language in order to communicate an overall image to us (see John 20:31). In writing their Gospels as they did, they sought to present the historical life of Christ within a theological setting. The simple fact is that there is no way that everything that Jesus said and did could have been recorded for us in written form. Therefore, the Gospel writers used the real historical events of Jesus' life and gave them an interpretive setting that allowed their readers to obtain an overall vision of Jesus Christ and His mission. (For more on the Gospels as historically accurate, see chapter 1 of Gerhard Lohfink's *Jesus of Nazareth*.[3])

"There are also many other things that Jesus did, but if these were to be described individually, I do not think the whole world would contain the books that would be written" (John 21:25).

All of this shows us that when the Gospel writers recounted healings and miracles, they were far more interested in presenting us with an image of Jesus as the embodiment of God's healing power than they were in sharing the details of how Jesus healed. The point of these stories is not merely to show us that miracles took place but to reveal

3   Gerhard Lohfink, *Jesus of Nazareth* (Michael Glazier Books, 2012).

to us one important truth: The Kingdom of God is at hand. The Gospel writers wanted to show us that God is present and active in history through His Son, Jesus Christ. This is why Jesus' miracles are often referred to as "signs." They are events that point us to a deeper truth: God is at work in the world. When Jesus healed people with leprosy, the point of the story (both for the writers and the readers) is not how the healing took place but what it meant that lepers had been healed. To live with leprosy meant living outside of the community; it meant being separated and isolated. In healing lepers Jesus isn't showing off His power, He is revealing His mission, a mission of reconciliation and restoration to community.

When we consider miracles today, it is important to approach them with a similar perspective. The meaning and significance of miracles should not be sought in the details of how the event occurred, but in the profound recognition of God's presence and activity in our lives. The truth is that God is always active, but we don't always recognize this. Asking, "Does this event have a natural or supernatural cause?" ultimately misses the point. It is in looking at the events of life through the eyes of faith that we come to recognize more and more God's presence and activity in the world. Think about it: Why was Jesus not able to perform any miracles in Nazareth (see Mark 6)? Was it because He was having a bad week and couldn't get His divine engine running? Of course not! The Bible says it was because of the people's lack of faith. The problem was one of faith, not of power. Miracles did not occur in Nazareth because the people there did not look at Jesus' ministry through the eyes of faith. When we seek to see as God sees, we come to recognize the miraculous all around us. Through faith we come to see that the Kingdom of God is truly at hand.

"For believers, the Biblical stories are not about what happened at the beginning of time or about what happened to another people at another time. They are about what God is doing in the present. God's creative activity is still going on, but to discern that activity requires the faith of a person willing to see beyond phenomena" (Leslie J. Hoppe, O.F.M., *Priests, Prophets and Sages*, 109).

CHAPTER 11

I COULD NEVER BELONG TO A RELIGION THAT HATES GAY PEOPLE.

Before delving into this issue, it is important that we say a few words about the term "gay." This term is used here because of its common use by people today to describe those with same-sex attraction. It must be clearly stated that the use of the term in the chapter heading is not meant to be derogatory or demeaning in any way. It is simply used as a reflection of how questions of same-sex attraction are commonly framed. While people's sexual orientation is certainly a part of who they are, we recognize that this orientation does not define them or capture the totality of their identity.

The belief that Catholicism embraces or advocates any sort of hatred toward people with same-sex attraction is both tragic and inaccurate. At its core, the Christian faith is rooted in love, and in an invitation to share in the very life and goodness of the Trinity — an invitation that extends to *all*. In the Christian worldview, no one is rejected, no one is excluded, and certainly no one is hated. So where does the idea that the Church hates homosexuals come from? There are two likely explanations for this view: (1) an insufficient understanding of the Church's teaching on homosexuality and same-sex "marriage" and (2) an improper and unloving presentation of the Church's teaching on these issues by Christians themselves.

With regard to the first explanation, there are really two issues involved: homosexuality itself and the question of marriage between people of the same sex. Before examining the question of marriage, let's look at homosexuality in general.

WHAT EXACTLY DOES THE CHURCH TEACH?
In order to properly frame the Church's teaching, it must be clearly stated that the Church understands reality to have an ordered, purposeful design. This is true of human life in all of its aspects: personal, social, economic, and political. Because God created the

world with a purpose — to experience the fullness of life-giving love and communion — all of these aspects of human life must function to move people in the direction intended by God. This also is true of personal relationships, including human sexuality. It is a fact of reality (entirely independent of the Catholic faith) that humanity consists of men and women. Given this fact and the fact that God created the world to move according to a purposeful design, we must ask the question: Why did God create humanity as male and female?

Surely God *could* have created humans (or whatever they would be called) with only one gender who could have perpetuated their species in whatever way God designed — maybe in this case a stork really would bring babies! But God chose to make us male and female, and it is only through the union of male and female that the human species is able to continue throughout history. This is not a statement of faith or an ideological viewpoint; this is an anthropological and biological fact: Every human being to ever exist is the result of the sexual union of their mother and father. This doesn't provide an answer to why God made us male and female, but it does give us an answer to the significance of this fact for the human race. God made us male and female because this is the way that He intended to perpetuate humanity's existence throughout history. There is simply no other way for human beings to guarantee their own existence over time. And this union is so fundamental to our existence as human beings that every culture throughout history has held up the family as the essential core of society.

Within the family (defined as the union of man and woman and any children that come from that union), new generations are given life, raised and formed in the values and traditions of their society, and continue humanity's presence through time. And because of this, the institution of marriage has always been held in great honor. Again, this is not a religious viewpoint; this is a fact of history. In every culture throughout history, no relationship was more vital and central to the very existence of that culture as the relationship between man and woman and any child born from their union.

But there is more to the story, and this is where revelation comes in. When the Church looks at the language of Sacred Scripture, it discovers that being made male and female is an essential part of what being made in the "image and likeness" of God is all about. The relationship between man and woman in marriage and the new life that it brings is a reflection of God Himself, who is essentially a family, a life-giving communion of persons. And it is for this reason that the Church has constantly upheld the dignity and nature of marriage.

SAME-SEX ATTRACTION
AND THE SACRAMENT OF MATRIMONY

What does all of this have to do with homosexuality? One of the most heavily debated issues in the U.S. today is the question of whether or not marriage should be redefined in a way that would allow people of the same sex to get married. As you have probably seen, the Church has been active in seeking to prevent traditional marriage from being redefined. The two issues here are homosexuality in general and how marriage ought to be defined.

Regarding homosexuality, the Catholic Church teaches that, in creating humanity as male and female, God wrote into our very nature the truth that men and woman are meant to enter into a covenant relationship that brings communion and new life. Men and women were made for each other, and the differences in the sexes are ultimately complementary. Another way of saying this is that man and woman are *ordered* to each other. By "ordered," we mean that men and women were designed for a complementary union, a union that has its fullest expression within the context of marriage.

Marriage is the institution that seeks to uphold this unique and essential relationship for humanity. With this in mind, the Church says that homosexual acts are "intrinsically disordered" (*CCC* 2357). While this may come across as very harsh, what it means is that homosexual acts are contrary to how God has designed (or ordered) human sexuality. This is not a judgment of character (or it shouldn't be); it is an assessment of how the use of something measures up to its intended purpose. For example, if I use a chair as a golf club, I am using it in a way that is contrary to its intended purpose, so you could say it is a *disordered* use of the chair. In a similar way, human sexuality has a purpose — to bring unity to husband and wife through a mutual gift of self and bring about the possibility of new life and the continuation of mankind.

Someone might ask, "But what about people who have a same-sex attraction? Are you calling them disordered?" The first response is that *all humanity* is disordered. Because of sin, our very nature has been wounded and is therefore disordered; we tend to want and seek things that are contrary to what God intends for us. Any inclination that we have that is contrary to God's plan and design for humanity is disordered, and all of us possess the marks of this disordered, fallen nature. The Church is very aware that for most people, their same-sex attraction is not something of their own choosing; it is simply a part of who they are. This fact should not be trivialized, and it would be unfair of the Church to have a "just snap out of it" mentality toward those with same-sex attraction.

The Church teaches that persons with same-sex attraction are, like all of humanity, persons made in the image and likeness of God and are destined for eternal communion with Him. The Church also teaches that a distinction must be made between homosexual orientation and homosexual acts. To have a same-sex attraction is not in itself sinful, but sexual acts outside of God's design for human sexuality are. Any time we use our sexuality in ways that are contrary to God's design is using them in a disordered and therefore sinful way. This is where we have to be careful. We can't just single out homosexual acts as being the only thing outside of God's plan for sexuality. Any use of human sexuality (by homosexuals or heterosexuals) that is contrary to God's design for humanity is a disordered use of our sexuality.

GOD'S PLAN FOR MARRIAGE

The Catholic Church teaches that human sexuality is only carried out in its proper design when done within the context of a free, lifelong, faithful, and fruitful union of a man and woman — namely, marriage. It is only within the confines of marriage that human sexuality is able to fulfill what God intended it to be. At the heart of the Church's perspective is the view that marriage has an essential nature, and this nature can only be discovered; it is not something we created. It is part of a planned design on the part of God and thus not something we are free to redefine.

This is the real issue: The Church is opposed to any effort to redefine marriage as the public recognition of the commitment between two individuals for their fulfillment. Why? Because the Church is opposed to any

"The intimate community of life and love which constitutes the married state has been established by the Creator and endowed with its own proper laws [...] God Himself is the author of marriage. The vocation to marriage is written in the very nature of man and woman as they came from the hand of the Creator" (*CCC* 1603).

understanding of marriage that would make it less than what it actually is. The proposed redefinition makes marriage ultimately about the self-fulfillment of adults. Unfortunately, this is precisely the understanding of marriage had by most people, and it has led to a marriage and family crisis in our country — a crisis (and this is the important part) for which *heterosexuals* are to blame. You see, it is heterosexuals who have largely bought into this understanding of marriage, with the result that as soon as marriage becomes challenging and demands sacrifice, it is quickly abandoned. As soon as one spouse no longer feels fulfilled, he or she begins to look for a way out.

Often the same-sex marriage discussion is presented like this: If we allow same-sex couples to marry, it will destroy marriage and the family. The way it should really go is this: Marriage and the family are in ruins, and if we redefine marriage to be nothing more than the public recognition of a commitment between couples, it will only further the problem. Why? Because this definition shifts the focus of marriage onto the self. Ultimately, marriage becomes for *my* fulfillment and meeting *my* needs. Redefining marriage won't cause this perspective of marriage; the call to redefine marriage is a result of people having already bought into this perspective. And it is *heterosexuals* who have almost universally bought in to this, the result of which has been an overall breakdown of marriage and the family.

FAMILY MATTERS

The essential point here is that there is a marriage and family breakdown in America and attempts to redefine marriage will only make this problem worse. The proposed redefinition places the focus on the individual, saying ultimately personal fulfillment is at the heart of marriage. Marriage has become, for the most part, about what *I* get out of it. The negative effects of this view of marriage on our overall understanding of relationships can be seen everywhere: In the promiscuity of the "hook-up" culture and one-night stands, in the high divorce rate, in the number of single parent homes, in families with one or both parents absent, and in the rate of adultery and infidelity. And the Church is opposed to anything that might perpetuate this problem, such as changing the very definition of marriage in a way that embodies this mentality.

An additional problem with this understanding of marriage is that it is silent with regard to children. As it stands now, marriage is the *only* institution that unites spouses to each other *and* any children that come from their union. When we look at marriage from the perspective of children (every single one of whom has a mother and father), it is important for there to be some institution that safeguards the rights of children to be united to their father *and* mother. But here's the thing: An institution like this already exists. It's called marriage, which unites husband and wife to each other and any children born from their union.

This institution needs to be *strengthened* if we are to overcome the current decline of marriage and the family. And redefining marriage in a way that takes individual fulfillment as its starting point would undo the one institution that exists to secure the rights of children to be united to their mother and father. (For a more complete discussion of this I *highly* recommend the book *Getting the Marriage Conversation Right: A Guide for Effective Dialogue*, by William B. May.)

The Church doesn't say that people of the same sex shouldn't be *allowed* to get married; the Church says that people of the same sex are *incapable* of marriage. That's why there is a push to *redefine* marriage. The current definition of marriage makes it impossible for same-sex couples to participate in it. But as we said before, marriage has a particular nature and essence, and this nature can only be discovered, never redefined. The current definition of marriage reflects the essential nature of marriage. We are not free to redefine the nature of marriage any more than we are free to redefine the nature of a human person. So what about same-sex couples? The reality of people of the same sex entering into relationships is simply a part of life, and the Church is not advocating making such relationships punishable by law. Ultimately, people are free to do what they wish with their lives. Part of what it means to be human is having the ability to freely direct our lives as we choose.

What the Church is opposed to is *redefining* marriage to accommodate these relationships. It is important that we realize this. The key issue in the current discussion is *not* the morality of homosexual behavior; the Church is not out to criminalize same-sex relationships. The key issue is whether or not marriage should be redefined. The Church is interested in strengthening marriage and the family, and any redefinition of marriage that makes the personal fulfillment of adults the central focus will only further the problem. While it may seem like the Church is trying to *withhold* something from same-sex couples, in reality, the Church is trying to *uphold* something — the one institution that unites men and women to each other and any children that result from their union.

THE CALL FOR US ALL

All of this leaves us with one important question: What about people who are both Catholic and have homosexual tendencies? The Church says that they, *like all people*, are called to chastity. What is chastity? It is the right use, in mind and action, of our human sexuality. Chastity means expressing our sexuality in ways that are consistent with God's design for humanity.

Unfortunately, people often think that chastity is only for single people; once you are married you get to leave chastity behind. This is entirely wrong. *Everyone* is called to chastity, but this chastity will look differently for each person depending upon their vocation and state in life. A priest living out chastity involves celibacy (no sex) as well as keeping his mind and heart pure of lust and temptation. A married person's chastity will obviously not involve celibacy (it is an essential part of marriage to engage in sex — what the Church calls "the marital embrace"). Chastity in marriage means fidelity (no adultery), mutual consent (force or compulsion is always a violation of chastity), openness to life, honoring periods of abstinence for various reasons, and guarding the mind and heart from lust and temptation. Married couples aren't off the hook when it comes to chastity. Chastity is part of what it means to be Catholic, whether you are married, single, ordained, or religious.

What will chastity look like for Catholics with a same-sex attraction? The same thing It looks like for any unmarried person. It involves celibacy, maintaining healthy relationships, and seeking purity in mind and heart. Sex outside of marriage is sex outside of marriage, whether you are homosexual or heterosexual. Homosexuals, like heterosexuals, are called to holiness in thought and action, a holiness that necessarily involves chastity.

One of the reasons the Church's views on homosexuality and "same-sex marriage" are not well received is that there appears to be (at times accurately) an uneven focus on homosexuality to the exclusion of the numerous other violations of chastity present in society. In his book *Bad Religion*, Ross Douthat says that the Church's message must be "moralistic but also holistic."[4] This means that it would be a mistake for the Church to focus exclusively on homosexuality when it comes to sexual morality without raising the bar equally high for heterosexuals who fail to live in chastity.

> "One reason the Christian insistence of chastity for homosexuals seems particularly cruel and unreasonable is that the Christian churches no longer successfully hold up heterosexual chastity as a clearly defined, successfully lived out ideal."[5]

---

4   Ross Douthat, *Bad Religion: How We Became a Nation of Heretics* (Free Press, 2012), 288.
5   Ibid., 290.

What is needed is a Church that sets the same moral standards of chastity for *all* its members. As we said before, it is the *heterosexual* lapse into selfishness, adultery, pornography, contraception, and casual sex that has caused and perpetuated the marriage crisis. If the Church's voice on sexual morality is going to be accepted with credibility, it must be consistent in presenting the Gospel call of chastity to all people (which is exactly what the Church professes in her teaching — see *CCC* 2348).

As we conclude this chapter, let's not minimize the fact that homosexuality is a difficult issue for people both inside and outside the Church. And as we address this issue, it is important to keep a few things in mind:

> (1) *The Church is not foreign to anyone.* Everyone is welcome and should find a home in the Church. This doesn't mean that the Church should have an anything goes view of life, but if our message to the world is ultimately one of "if you're gay, you don't belong," then we are living in serious contradiction to the Gospel.

> (2) *The current debate about same-sex unions should focus on the issue of redefining marriage, not the morality of sexual acts between people of the same sex.* The Church's motivation in preserving the current definition of marriage is to strengthen the institution of marriage, which has been greatly weakened by society's failure to live according to God's design for marriage.

> (3) *Any dehumanizing language or mistreatment of people with same-sex attraction must be rejected as fundamentally opposed to the Gospel.* The Church does not "hate gay people." If our words and actions send this message, then we must seriously reassess them. The Church must be a refuge for all people, a place where people are welcomed as they are. But it must also be a place where our minds are illuminated and our wills are strengthened, so that our lives, which have been disordered by sin, can be transformed and progress toward perfection.

WHAT IS FAITH?

There is one central concept that has continued to come up throughout this book: faith. Since it is important that when we use a term we actually take the time to define it, we will end this book with an overview of the way the Catholic Church understands the word *faith*.

Sometimes the Church will use the term *faith* to refer to "the Faith," meaning all that God has revealed and entrusted to the Catholic Church for the salvation of the world. God reveals Himself so we can know Him, and in knowing Him come to love Him. This *revelation* of God is what constitutes "the faith" of the Church. And the Church continues to pass on "the faith" to each generation, so that all people might have access to God's saving truth throughout history.

The word *faith* has also been used throughout this book to refer to a form of *knowledge*. Traditionally, the Church speaks of three ways of knowing God. These three ways are often referred to as three "lights" by which we can see God: the light of reason, the light of faith, and the light of glory. Let's look at these separately.

THE LIGHT OF REASON

The light of reason refers to that knowledge we're able to gain through the use of our minds alone. Through reason we can discover certain truths about the natural world (science). We can discover truths about how we are to live in relation to others (ethics). We can know truths about the nature of things like knowledge and logic (philosophy). And we can even use human reason to arrive at knowledge of the existence of God and the nature of the soul (metaphysics). The fact of the matter is that human reason is quite a powerful gift, and through it there is a great deal that we can know, including knowing that God exists. This knowledge of God through the use of our minds is what the Church calls knowledge by the light of reason.

THE LIGHT OF FAITH

The light of faith refers to that knowledge we are able to gain through faith in what God reveals. Before going further, let's talk about divine revelation for a moment. Ultimately, divine revelation is God revealing *Himself*. God, through a free gift, chose to make Himself known to His creation. St. Thomas Aquinas said that God is goodness itself, and that it is the very nature of goodness to want to be shared. God didn't need to reveal Himself to us (just as He didn't need to create us in the first place), but He freely chose to do so because He wanted us to know Him and experience His love. As John Paul II put it, we were made *by love and for love* (see *Familiaris Consortio*, 11). Ultimately, God revealed Himself to us so that we could know how to live in communion with Him. Through divine revelation God extends an invitation to us to share in His own life. This is what God wants for all people — to know Him, love Him, and live eternally with Him. Through divine revelation, God shows us the path that leads to Himself.

> "It pleased God, in His goodness and wisdom, to reveal Himself and to make known the mystery of His will. His will was that men should have access to the Father, through Christ, the Word made flesh, in the Holy Spirit, and thus become sharers in the divine nature" (*Dei Verbum*, 2).

Now, where does the light of faith come in? As we saw in chapter 9, there are some things that reason simply cannot tell us. We cannot know through reason that God is a Trinity, or that Jesus Christ is the incarnate Word of God, or that the sacraments give us the grace necessary to make our way to heaven. Furthermore, even those things that we *can* know through reason are often known with great difficulty and with a mixture of truth and error. Therefore, God wanted to provide us with a further light by which we could see the truth: the light

> "Faith is certain. It is more certain than all human knowledge because it is founded on the very word of God who cannot lie. To be sure, revealed truths can seem obscure to human reason and experience, but the certainty that the divine light gives is greater than that which the light of natural reason gives" (*CCC* 157).

of faith. Through faith in what God has revealed, we come to know the truth about God and about how we are to live as His children. And this knowledge of God is *really* knowledge. Through faith we can know that God is a Trinity. Through faith we can know that God gives us the grace to become His children through the Sacrament of Baptism. Why? Because He has revealed this to us. And since God is truth itself, we know that what He reveals to be true *is true*. In fact, as we saw earlier, this knowledge through faith is *more certain* than the knowledge that comes through reason. Why? Because it depends not on our own minds, but on the reliability of the One revealing Himself, God. Therefore, when it comes to our knowledge of God, we are able to see God more clearly through the light of faith than we are through the light of reason. However, both of these lights fall short of the knowledge of God that we will one day have through the light of glory.

THE LIGHT OF GLORY

Through reason, we can know that God exists. Through faith we can know that God is a family, and that we are invited to become His adopted children by grace. Through the light of glory, we will be able to know God as He is *in His very essence*. This might seem like an odd phrase, but it comes from the language of St. Paul, who says that one day we will see God *face to face*. Now, obviously, God doesn't have a face, but the idea behind this image is that through the light of glory, we will be able to see God as He really is.

> "At present we see indistinctly, as in a mirror, but then face to face. At present I know partially; then I shall know fully, as I am fully known" (1 Corinthians 13:12).

This knowledge of God through the light of glory is what all those who are in heaven have. That's why it is called the light of *glory*; it's the knowledge that those who have lived and died with Christ in this life have in the glory of heaven. Another term for this way of seeing God is the *beatific vision*, which refers to the joy of seeing and knowing God in all His glory. We really don't know what this will be like. St. Paul tells us that we can't even begin to imagine it (see 1 Corinthians 2:9). And when this day comes, faith will be no more. Why? Because faith is the hope and assurance of things to come. Once we come to possess that for which we have hope, we will have no further need for faith. Therefore, the light of faith finds its ultimate fulfillment in the light of glory, which replaces and surpasses the light of faith.

THE ACT OF FAITH

So far we have talked about faith in terms of "the faith," meaning, all that God has revealed and entrusted to the Church for the salvation of the world. We have also discussed faith as a type of knowledge, a light by which we are able to see God. The last thing we must do is talk about faith as an *act*. Here's a simple (or at least brief) way of defining the *act of faith*: Faith is an act of the *intellect*, moved by the *will*, inspired by *grace*. Crystal clear, right?

Let's see if we can break this down a bit. Faith is an act of the intellect, meaning that it is something that occurs in the mind. Faith is a response in our mind (called *assent*) to what is revealed. "Assent" here means saying, "Yes, I believe" to something proposed to us. For example, Jesus tells us that He is the way, the truth, and the life, and that no one comes to the Father except through Him. We can either accept or reject this statement. When we accept it as true (giving the *assent of faith*), our minds say, "Yes, I believe" (which, by the way, is what we are saying every time we say, "Amen"). Through faith, our mind (or intellect) accepts what is presented to it for belief as true.

Faith, therefore, is an act of the intellect. However, it is not *just* an act of the intellect. Faith is an act of the intellect *that is moved by the will*. Our will tells our intellect to give assent to what is revealed. Now, why is the will involved here? Because the will tells us to put our trust in the One revealing Himself to us. The will tells us that the One speaking to us is worthy of our assent.

You see, when it comes to human reason, our intellect is convinced solely by the evidence in front of us. For example, when we are presented with the proposition "two plus two equals four," once we understand what it means for there to be two of something added to two more of something, we are fully convinced of the truth of the claim that "two plus two equals four." We don't need our will to tell us to assent to this; our mind tells us that we must. In a certain sense, once we understand the first part of the equation (two plus two) we can't help but accept the conclusion (equals four).

"In faith, the human intellect and will cooperate with divine grace: believing is an act of the intellect assenting to the divine truth by command of the will moved by God through grace" (*CCC* 155).

With divine revelation, it's a different story. The truths of divine revelation are not fully evident to us, and so we must place our faith in their truthfulness. And it is our will that tells us to do this. Not because the claim appears true to us, but because of the trustworthiness of the One revealing the truth. Therefore, in faith, our will tells our intellect to accept what is proposed for us to believe because of the reliability of the revealer.

Now, this is only possible by grace, which inspires and enables us to put our trust in God who is revealing Himself. In faith, grace comes to our aid in order to help us to confidently submit ourselves to the trustworthiness of what God has revealed. This means that faith is a unique action on our part. Through faith, our will tells our mind that what is being proposed to us is trustworthy, not because it appears to be true to our mind, but because God is a trustworthy source. This also means that faith involves our entire being. Faith isn't just accepting something as true (believing that God exists); it is also an act of surrendering our entire life to the One in whom we place our trust and committing ourselves to live according to the truth that He sets before us (believing in God's path to salvation).

> "Because God is trustworthy, it is reasonable to have faith in Him, to stand fast on His word" (*Lumen Fidei*, 23).

This is why St. Paul speaks of faith in terms of "the obedience of faith" (Romans 1:5; 16:26). Faith necessarily involves a way of life. This is why the Church holds up the lives of the saints as a model for us to follow. As Pope Francis said, "If we want to understand what faith is, we need to follow the route it has taken" (*Lumen Fidei*, 8). By looking at the way in which faith has been lived out in the past, we can see how it is meant to provide a compass that leads the way to the light of glory. This is also why St. Paul, after giving the famous definition of faith as "the realization of what is hoped for and evidence of things not seen" (Hebrews 11:1), walks us through the great faith and trust of those who came before Christ. At its core, faith is a way of life — a way that places its full trust in God as the fullness of truth, the only path to true happiness, and the ultimate fulfillment of our every desire.

This entire book has been about debunking the main reasons people reject God, Catholicism, and faith. Many people in the world today view faith and religion as obstacles to human happiness. But what has been the fruit of this rejection of faith? People have looked for meaning and fulfillment in everything but God, and what they have found is discontent. Why? Because, as St. Augustine said, we were made for God, and our hearts are restless until they rest in Him. Money, power, fame, and passing pleasures cannot give us the ultimate satisfaction that we seek. And yet, so often we turn away from God, thinking that the really good stuff is to be found elsewhere. This has led to a crisis of meaning. Without God as the ultimate reason for our existence, we can easily pass from moment to moment without any sense of direction. Faith, on the other hand, gives us a taste in advance of the life for which we were made: To know and love God and to live in communion with Him and each other for eternity. Through faith we orient our life toward its proper end. A life of faith is not easy, but it is the only life that will ultimately satisfy us. God has extended an invitation to us; what will be our response? Let's close with these words from Pope Francis:

> Once man has lost the fundamental orientation which unifies his existence, he breaks down into the multiplicity of his desires; in refusing to await the time of promise, his life-story disintegrates into a myriad of unconnected instants. Idolatry, then, is always polytheism, an aimless passing from one lord to another. Idolatry does not offer a journey but rather a plethora of paths leading nowhere and forming a vast labyrinth. Those who choose not to put their trust in God must hear the din of countless idols crying out: "Put your trust in me!"
>
> Faith, tied as it is to conversion, is the opposite of idolatry; it breaks with idols to turn to the living God in a personal encounter. Believing means entrusting oneself to a merciful love which always accepts and pardons, which sustains and directs our lives, and which shows its power by its ability to make straight the crooked lines of our history. Faith consists in the willingness to let ourselves be constantly transformed and renewed by God's call. Herein lies the paradox: By constantly turning toward the Lord, we discover a sure path, which liberates us from the dissolution imposed upon us by idols (*Lumen Fidei*, 13).

MOVING FORWARD
STAYING CATHOLIC IN COLLEGE

The perfect gift for graduating seniors! The transition out of high school for a Catholic teen is a defining moment, simply because their faith will be tested. This book is aimed towards graduating seniors (and anyone still adjusting to the college scene) in hopes that as they move forward, their faith will move with them. The book includes practical wisdom on how to successfully transition into college and not only survive but thrive in their Catholic faith.

Topics: The book covers 60 topics with timely insight on how to deal with everything from challenging roommates to handling homesickness to finances and study habits. The book also doesn't shy away from hard-hitting subjects like dealing with addictions, failure, and relationships gone wrong.

Authors: Over 30 writers contributed to *Moving Forward: Staying Catholic in College.* Some writers are still in college today, but other writers are older and have had years to reflect on their college experience. Because of their unique points of view, the finished book is both fresh and timeless. Key writers include Mark Hart (Catholic author, speaker, and radio personality), Jackie Francois (Catholic speaker and recording artist), and Matt Smith (Catholic speaker and blogger).

Paperback 5.5"x8.5", 152 pages,

$12.00

WORTH THE WAIT
A CATHOLIC TEEN'S GUIDE
TO DATING, MARRIAGE, AND HAPPINESS

Worth the Wait is a compilation of blogs, reflections, and insight from some of the best minds and loving hearts working in Catholic youth ministry to help teens navigate through what the world tries to tell them about love and relationships. Because choosing to live out chastity is not simply about saying "no" today; it's about saying "yes" to tomorrow, and forever. Chastity isn't always easy, but it is *Worth the Wait*.

Paperback, 5.5"x 8.5", 208 pages,

$14.00

LifeTeen.com